ALPHABETICAL LISTING OF PHILOS

Abelard, Peter	1079–1142
Al-Ghazali	1058–1111
Anaxagoras	500–428 B.C.
Anaximander	c. 610–545 B.C.
Anaximenes	c. 580–500 B.C.
Anselm, Saint	1033–1109
Aquinas, Saint Thomas	1225–1274
Aristotle	384–322 B.C.
Augustine, Saint	354–430
Austin, John	1911–1960
Averroës	1126–1198
Avicenna	980–1037
Ayer, A. J.	1910–1989
Bacon, Francis	1561–1626
Beauvoir, Simone de	1908–1986
Bentham, Jeremy	1748–1832
Bergson, Henri	1859–1941
Berkeley, George	1685–1753
Boethius	c. 480–524
Carnap, Rudolph	1891–1970
Comte, Auguste	1798–1857
Copernicus, Nicholas	1473–1543
Darwin, Charles	1809–1882
Democritus	c. 460–360 B.C.
Derrida, Jacques	1930–
Descartes, René	1596–1650
Dewey, John	1859–1952
Dostoevsky, Fyodor	1821–1881
Eckhart, Meister	c. 1260–1327
Einstein, Albert	1879–1955
Empedocles	c. 495–435 B.C.
Engels, Friedrich	1820–1895
Epictetus	c. 50–138
Epicurus	341–270 B.C.
Erasmus, Desiderius	1466–1536
Erigena, John Scotus	c. 810–877
Foucault, Michel	1926–1984
Freud, Sigmund	1856–1939
Galileo	1564–1642
Gorgias	c. 483–375 B.C.
Hegel, Georg W. F.	1770–1831
Heidegger, Martin	1889–1976
Heraclitus	c. 540–480 B.C.
Hobbes, Thomas	1588–1679
Hume, David	1711–1776
Husserl, Edmund	1859–1938
James, William	1842–1910
Kant, Immanuel	1724–1804
Kierkegaard, Søren	1813–1855
Leibniz, Gottfried	1646–1716
Locke, John	1632–1704
Luther, Martin	1483–1546
Maimonides, Moses	1135–1204
Marx, Karl	1818–1883
Mill, John Stuart	1806–1873
Newton, Sir Isaac	1642–1727
Nietzsche, Friedrich	1844–1900
Ockham, William of	c. 1280–1349
Parmenides	c. 515–450 B.C.
Pascal, Blaise	1623–1662
Peirce, Charles S.	1839–1914
Plato	c. 428–348 B.C.
Plotinus	205–270
Protagoras	c. 490–420 B.C.
Pyrrho	c. 360–270 B.C.
Pythagoras	c. 570–495 B.C.
Quine, Willard V. O.	1908–2000
Rorty, Richard	1931–
Rousseau, Jean Jacques	1712–1778
Russell, Bertrand	1872–1970
Ryle, Gilbert	1900–1976
Sartre, Jean-Paul	1905–1980
Schopenhauer, Arthur	1788–1860
Scotus, John Duns	c. 1266–1308
Socrates	c. 470–399 B.C.
Spinoza, Benedict (Baruch)	1632–1677
Thales	624–545 B.C.
Voltaire	1694–1778
Whitehead, Alfred North	1861–1947
Wittgenstein, Ludwig	1889–1951
Xenophanes	c. 570–478 B.C.
Zeno the Eleatic	c. 490–430 B.C.
Zeno the Stoic	c. 336–264 B.C.

CHRONOLOGICAL LIST OF PHILOSOPHERS

THE ANCIENT PERIOD

Thales	c. 624–545	B.C.
Anaximander	c. 610–545	B.C.
Anaximenes	c. 580–500	B.C.
Pythagoras	c. 570–495	B.C.
Xenophanes	c. 570–478	B.C.
Heraclitus	c. 540–480	B.C.
Parmenides	c. 515–450	B.C.
Anaxagoras	500–428	B.C.
Empedocles	c. 495–435	B.C.
Zeno the Eleatic	c. 490–430	B.C.
Protagoras	c. 490–420	B.C.
Gorgias	c. 483–375	B.C.
Socrates	c. 470–399	B.C.
Democritus	c. 460–360	B.C.
Plato	c. 428–348	B.C.
Aristotle	384–322	B.C.
Pyrrho	c. 360–270	B.C.
Epicurus	341–270	B.C.
Zeno the Stoic	c. 336–264	B.C.
Epictetus	c. 50–138	
Plotinus	205–270	

THE MIDDLE AGES

Augustine, Saint	354–430
Boethius	c. 480–524
Erigena, John Scotus	c. 810–877
Anselm, Saint	1033–1109
Avicenna	980–1037
Al-Ghazali	1058–1111
Abelard, Peter	1079–1142
Averroës	1126–1198
Maimonides, Moses	1135–1204
Aquinas, Saint Thomas	1225–1274
Eckhart, Meister	c. 1260–1327
Scotus, John Duns	c. 1266–1308
Ockham, William of	c. 1280–1349

THE MODERN PERIOD

Erasmus, Desiderius	1466–1536
Copernicus, Nicholas	1473–1543
Luther, Martin	1483–1546
Bacon, Francis	1561–1626
Galileo	1564–1642
Hobbes, Thomas	1588–1679
Descartes, René	1596–1650
Pascal, Blaise	1623–1662
Spinoza, Benedict (Baruch)	1632–1677
Locke, John	1632–1704
Newton, Sir Isaac	1642–1727
Leibniz, Gottfried	1646–1716
Berkeley, George	1685–1753
Voltaire	1694–1778
Hume, David	1711–1776
Rousseau, Jean Jacques	1712–1778
Kant, Immanuel	1724–1804
Bentham, Jeremy	1748–1832
Hegel, Georg W. F.	1770–1831
Schopenhauer, Arthur	1788–1860
Comte, Auguste	1798–1857
Mill, John Stuart	1806–1873
Darwin, Charles	1809–1882
Kierkegaard, Søren	1813–1855
Marx, Karl	1818–1883
Engels, Friedrich	1820–1895
Dostoevsky, Fyodor	1821–1881
Nietzsche, Friedrich	1844–1900

THE CONTEMPORARY PERIOD

Peirce, Charles S.	1839–1914
James, William	1842–1910
Freud, Sigmund	1856–1939
Husserl, Edmund	1859–1938
Bergson, Henri	1859–1941
Dewey, John	1859–1952
Whitehead, Alfred North	1861–1947
Russell, Bertrand	1872–1970
Einstein, Albert	1879–1955
Wittgenstein, Ludwig	1889–1951
Heidegger, Martin	1889–1976
Carnap, Rudolph	1891–1970
Ryle, Gilbert	1900–1976
Sartre, Jean-Paul	1905–1980
Beauvoir, Simone de	1908–1986
Quine, Willard V. O.	1908–2000
Ayer, A. J.	1910–1989
Austin, John	1911–1960
Foucault, Michel	1926–1984
Derrida, Jacques	1930–
Rorty, Richard	1931–

THE VOYAGE OF DISCOVERY

A HISTORICAL INTRODUCTION TO PHILOSOPHY

THE MEDIEVAL VOYAGE
100–1400

SECOND EDITION

William F. Lawhead
University of Mississippi

WADSWORTH

™
THOMSON LEARNING

Australia • Canada • Mexico • Singapore • Spain
United Kingdom • United States

WADSWORTH
THOMSON LEARNING

Publisher: Eve Howard
Philosophy Editor: Peter Adams
Assistant Editor: Kara Kindstrom
Editorial Assistant: Chalida Anusasananan
Marketing Manager: Dave Garrison
Marketing Assistant: Adam Hofmann
Print/Media Buyer: Barbara Britton
Permissions Editor: Joohee Lee

Production Service: The Book Company
Text Designer: Wendy LaChance
Photo Researcher: Myrna Engler
Copy Editor: Jane Loftus
Cover Designer: Yvo Riezebos
Cover Image: Shinichi Eguchi/Photonica
Compositor: Thompson Type
Cover and Text Printer: R. R. Donnelley, Crawfordsville

Printed in the United States of America
1 2 3 4 5 6 7 05 04 03 02

Wadsworth/Thomson Learning
10 Davis Drive
Belmont, CA 94002-3098
USA

For more information about our products, contact us:
Thomson Learning Academic Resource Center
1-800-423-0563
http://www.wadsworth.com

International Headquarters
Thomson Learning
International Division
290 Harbor Drive, 2nd Floor
Stamford, CT 06902-7477
USA

UK/Europe/Middle East/South Africa
Thomson Learning
Berkshire House
168-173 High Holborn
London WC1V 7AA
United Kingdom

Asia
Thomson Learning
60 Albert Street, #15-01
Albert Complex
Singapore 189969

Canada
Nelson Thomson Learning
1120 Birchmount Road
Toronto, Ontario M1K 5G4
Canada

Library of Congress Cataloging-in-Publication Data
Lawhead, William F.
    The medieval voyage / William F. Lawhead.
        p. cm.
    Includes bibliographical references and index.
    ISBN 0-534-56157-8
    1. Philosophy, Medieval—History. I. Title.

B721 .L34 2001
189—dc21   2001045461

CONTENTS

PREFACE

This current volume belongs to a four-part paperback series that includes *The Ancient Voyage, The Medieval Voyage, The Modern Voyage,* and *The Contemporary Voyage.* Each of these four volumes focuses on one particular period in the history of philosophy and represents one of the parts of the complete one-volume work *The Voyage of Discovery: A Historical Introduction to Philosophy* 2nd ed. It is hoped that publishing the book in multiple formats will make it more flexible and will increase its usefulness for instructors. Those who are teaching a particular historical period can use the appropriate paperback volume or volumes for that time period. This makes it cost effective to use my historical discussions with a collection of primary source readings. On the other hand, some will prefer to use the complete one-volume work for an introduction to philosophy course that covers significant thinkers from the Greeks to the contemporary period. Others (like me) teach a topically organized introduction course and follow that with one or two courses that survey the history of philosophy, using the complete *The Voyage of Discovery.*

This book has grown out of my thirty years of teaching the history of Western philosophy. I love to teach this subject. I have found that the history of philosophy develops students' critical thinking skills. After journeying with the course for awhile and following the point and counterpoint movements of the great historical debates, students begin to show a flare for detecting the assumptions, strengths, problems, and implications of a thinker's position. Furthermore, the history of philosophy provides students with an arsenal of essential terms, distinctions, categories, and critical questions for making sense out of the barrage of ideas they encounter in history, literature, psychology, politics, and even on television.

One reward of teaching philosophy is to see students develop new confidence in themselves on finding a kindred spirit in one or more of the great minds of history, who agree with their own assessment of what is fallacious or sound. By exposing students to unfamiliar viewpoints that are outrageous, fascinating, perplexing, hopeful, dangerous, gripping, troubling, and exhilarating, the history of philosophy helps them gain a renewed sense of childlike wonder, teaching them to look at the world with new eyes. Finally, throughout the history of philosophy, students often find ideas that are liberating and challenging, leading them down exciting paths that were not even on their conceptual maps when they started the course. I hope that this book will be an effective navigator's guide to such intellectual journeys.

GOALS THAT GUIDED THE WRITING OF THIS BOOK

After many years of teaching a course, a professor begins to get a sense of the "ideal" textbook. For me, an effective history of philosophy text should achieve the following goals:

1. Make the ideas of the philosophers as clear and accessible as possible to the average person. A student-friendly philosophy text will not read like an encyclopedia article, which contains dense but terse summaries of factual information.

2. Provide strategies for sorting out the overwhelming mass of contradictory ideas encountered in the history of philosophy.

3. Find the correct balance between the competing concerns of (a) technical accuracy versus accessibility and (b) breadth of scope versus depth of exposition.

4. Communicate the fact that philosophy is more than simply a collection of opinions on basic issues. Understanding a philosopher's arguments is just as important as the philosopher's conclusions.

5. Encourage the reader to evaluate the ideas discussed. The history of philosophy should be more than the intellectual equivalent of a wine-tasting party, where various philosophers are "sampled" simply to enjoy their distinct flavors.

Although that is certainly one of the delights of studying philosophy and should be encouraged, assessing the strengths and weaknesses of a philosopher's ideas is equally important.

6. Make clear the continuity of the centuries-long philosophical conversation. A course in the history of philosophy should not be like a display of different philosophical exhibits in glass cases. For me, the guiding image is philosophy as a big party where new conversations are continually starting up, while the themes of previous conversations are picked up and carried in different directions as new participants join the dialogue.

DISTINCTIVE FEATURES
OF THIS TEXT

• *A consistent structure is used.* For consistency and ease of comparison, the majority of chapters follow the same basic pattern:

1. The life and times of the philosopher

2. The major philosophical task that the philosopher tried to accomplish

3. Theory of knowledge

4. Metaphysics

5. Moral and political philosophy (when relevant)

6. Philosophy of religion (when relevant)

7. Evaluation and significance

• *Analysis of philosophical arguments is provided.* To emphasize that philosophy is a process and not just a set of results, I discuss the intellectual problems that motivated a philosopher's position and the reasons provided in its support. The book analyzes a number of explicitly outlined arguments of various philosophers, providing models of philosophical argumentation and analysis. In addition, I informally discuss numerous other arguments throughout the book.

• *The evaluation of ideas is stressed.* Most of the chapters end with a short evaluation of the philosophy discussed. These evaluations, however, are not presented as decisive "refutations" of the philosopher, which would relieve the reader of any

need to think further. Instead, the evaluations have been posed in terms of problems needing to be addressed and questions requiring an answer. Whenever possible, I have made this section a part of the historical dialogue by expressing the appraisals given by the philosopher's contemporaries and successors.

• *The significance of the ideas is emphasized.* The conclusion of each chapter also indicates the immediate and long-term significance of the philosopher's ideas and prepares the reader for the next turn in the historical dialogue. It makes clear the ways in which philosophical ideas can lead robust lives that continue far beyond their author's time.

• *The continuity between historical periods is emphasized.* Because each of the four paperback volumes represent a slice from the whole of Western philosophy, a special introductory chapter has been written that is specific to each of these four volumes. This chapter will situate the time period of that particular volume in terms of the philosophies that preceded it so that there will be no loss of continuity. Since *The Ancient Voyage* covers the beginnings of Western philosophy, the introductory chapter for that volume discusses the importance of studying the ancient Greeks. The introduction to *The Medieval Voyage* shows how that historical period arose out of the philosophies of the Greeks. In the introduction to *The Modern Voyage*, the shift from medieval thought is outlined in terms of four contrasts between the medieval and the modern outlook. Finally, *The Contemporary Voyage* begins with a brief overview of Immanuel Kant's philosophy and the various responses to it in the nineteenth century in order to set the stage for twentieth-century philosophy.

• *The philosophers are related to their cultural contexts.* In addition to these introductory chapters that emphasize the continuity with the thought that preceded the philosophies in each paperback volume, each major historical period covered by a particular paperback (Greek, early Christian to medieval, Renaissance and Reformation, Enlightenment, the nineteenth century, and the twentieth century) is introduced with a brief chapter discussing the intellectual-social milieu that provides the setting for the philosophies of that era. The questions addressed are: What were the dominant concerns and assumptions that animated each period in history? How did the different philosophers respond to the currents of thought of their time? and How did they influence their culture?

• *Diagrams.* Diagrams and tables provide visual representations of the elements of various philosophers' ideas.

• *Glossary.* A glossary is provided in which key terms used throughout the book are clearly and thoroughly defined. Words appearing in boldface in the text may be found in the glossary.

• *Questions for review and reflection.* At the end of each chapter are two lists of questions. The questions for understanding are more factual and enable the readers to review their understanding of the important ideas and terms. The questions for reflection require the readers to engage in philosophy by making their own evaluations of the philosopher's ideas, as well as working out their implications.

• *Instructor's manual.* In addition to the usual sections containing test questions and essay questions, this manual provides suggested topics for research papers, tips for introducing and motivating interest in each philosopher, chapter-by-chapter topics for discussion, and the contemporary implications of each philosopher's ideas.

SUGGESTED WAYS TO USE THIS BOOK

This book may be used with students who are already familiar with the leading issues and positions in philosophy and who now need to place these ideas in their historical context. However, since it does not assume any previous acquaintance with the subject, it may also be used to introduce students to philosophy for the first time, through the story of its history. I have tried to make clear that philosophy is an ongoing conversation, in which philosophers respond to the insights and shortcomings of their predecessors. Nevertheless, the chapters are self-contained enough that the instructor may put together a course that uses

selected chapters. For example, the chapter on Aquinas could be used as representative of medieval philosophy and Descartes used to represent the modern rationalists (skipping Spinoza and Leibniz). In the case of chapters that discuss a number of philosophers, only certain sections could be assigned. For example, to get a quick but partial glimpse of the wide range covered by analytic philosophy, the students could read only the sections on the early and later Wittgenstein. Although skipping over key thinkers is not ideal, teaching is a continual battle between time constraints and the desire to cover as much material in as much depth as possible.

The *Instructor's Manual* contains objective and essay questions that may be used in making up tests. In addition, Part 1 contains more reflective questions for discussion and essay assignments. I would encourage the instructor to make use of these questions in class in order to emphasize that philosophy is not a list of "who said what" but that it also involves the evaluation and application of the great ideas. Furthermore, because the students will have some of these topics and others posed as questions for reflection at the end of each chapter, they can be asked to have thought about their response to these questions prior to their discussion in class.

ABOUT THIS SECOND EDITION

I am gratified by the responses to the first edition of *The Voyage of Discovery* that I have received from professors using the book, from students who have been introduced to philosophy and its history through it, as well as from interested readers around the world who read it for personal enrichment. This second edition continues to have the distinctive features that so many enjoyed in the first edition and that have been highlighted in the previous sections of this preface. The subtitle has been changed to "A Historical Introduction to Philosophy" to communicate the fact that the book is intended to be used to introduce readers to philosophy for the first time as well as providing a comprehensive survey of Western philosophy. Besides some changes that have been made to aid in clarity and ease of reading, this current edition ends each chapter with questions to aid the reader in studying the material and in engaging in philosophical reflection on the ideas. Some of these questions have been taken from the essay and discussion questions in the *Instructor's Manual*. Nevertheless, over fifty percent of the essay questions in the *Instructor's Manual* remain unique to it. This edition is now available in two formats. As before, there is the one-volume edition that covers philosophy from the early Greeks to the contemporary period. New to the second edition is an alternative format that divides the book into four paperback volumes, corresponding to the four parts of the book. This makes it much more economical for the instructor to use parts of the book for courses that emphasize only particular time periods.

I hope that everyone who uses this book will find it both profitable and interesting. I encourage both professors and students to share with me their experience with the book as well as suggestions for improvement. Write to me at: Department of Philosophy, University of Mississippi, University, MS, 38677-1848. You may also send me e-mail at: wlawhead@olemiss.edu.

ACKNOWLEDGMENTS

From the initial, tentative outline of this book to the final chapter revisions, the manuscript has been extensively reviewed both by instructors who measured its suitability for the classroom and by scholars who reviewed its historical accuracy. Their comments have made it a much better book than the original manuscript. I take full responsibility, of course, for any remaining shortcomings. I am indebted to the following reviewers of this second edition: Jim Friel, State University New York—Farmingdale; John Longenay, University of Wisconsin—Riverside; Scott Lowe, Bloomsburg University; Michael Potts, Methodist College; and Blanche Premo-Hopkins, University of South Carolina—Aiken.

I also want to thank the reviewers of the first edition for their contributions: William Brown, Bryan College; Jill Buroker, California State University at San Bernardino; Bessie Chronaki, Central Piedmont Community College; Vincent Colapietro, Fordham University; Teresa Contrell, University of Louisville; Ronald Cox, San Antonio College; Timothy Davis, Essex Community College; Michelle Grier, University of San Diego; Eugene Lockwood, Oakton Community College; Michael Mendelson, University of California at San Diego; William Parent, Santa Clara University; Anthony Preus, State University of New York at Binghamton; Dennis Rothermel, California State University at Chico; James D. Ryan, Bronx Community College; James Spencer, Cuyahoga Community College; K. Sundaram, Lake Michigan College; Ken Stikkers, Seattle University; Robert Sweet, University of Dayton; Howard Tuttle, University of New Mexico; Jerome B. Wichelms, Jefferson Community College.

My thanks to the many people at the Wadsworth Publishing Company who played a role in the book's production. In particular, I appreciate the encouragement and support I received from Peter Adams, my editor.

The acknowledgments would be incomplete if I did not express my thanks to those individuals who have been particularly supportive throughout my career. My first exposure to philosophy was under the instruction of Arthur Holmes, my undergraduate chair, who ignited my love for the history of philosophy. The late Irwin C. Lieb guided me throughout my career as a graduate student, first as my professor, then as my department chair, and finally as graduate dean. Years of team teaching with David Schlafer, my former colleague, provided exciting lecture performances that have influenced what and how I teach. I have benefitted from good philosophical discussions with present and past colleagues, particularly Michael Harrington, Michael Lynch, Louis Pojman, and Robert Westmoreland. I also need to thank the many bright students who taught me how to teach.

This book is dedicated to my parents, James and Cecelia Lawhead, who first introduced me to the two dimensions of philosophy, love and wisdom; to my wife, Pam, who knows that love sometimes means being close and sometimes it means giving space; and to my sons, Joel and Andy, who taught me how much I do not know.

William Lawhead

Introduction to
The Medieval Voyage

This volume covers the philosophical thought of the Middle Ages or the medieval period. We begin with the rise of Christian philosophy in the first century of the Christian period and then spend a chapter on Augustine, who was one of the leading influences on medieval philosophy. From there we cover the various periods of medieval philosophy proper. Finally, this volume ends in the fourteenth century, with the thinkers and forces that began to unravel the tightly woven fabric of medieval thought and that gave birth to the Renaissance and modern philosophy.

As will be discussed later, designating this period of thought and culture as the "Middle Ages" (or *medieval* in Latin) was originally a term of abuse coined by the Renaissance thinkers who saw this period as a diversion or an unfortunate stagnant period of thought lodged between the greatness of ancient Greece and the Renaissance thinkers' own time. "Renaissance," of course, literally means "rebirth." Hence, it was thought that this age was a rebirth of all that was great in Greek civilization, in terms of its art, its literature, and its philosophy. What they did not realize was that this rebirth was indebted to the fertile soil that had been enriched

by much of medieval thought. That period of cultural and philosophical impoverishment known as the "Dark Ages" was only one portion of the thousand-year period constituting the Middle Ages.

Although the term "Middle Ages" stuck, and we continue to refer to this period by that name, we now have a more balanced assessment of the thought of this period. Certainly, there was much in medieval thought that limited the scope of human inquiry or misdirected it. Furthermore, while there were important, innovative scientists in the late medieval period, the rise of modern science came about when the medieval thinkers' assumptions about nature came into question. (These assumptions consisted of both the medieval thinkers' accounts of specific scientific facts as well as their broad, conceptual framework.) Having said this, however, the story of our intellectual history cannot be told without an understanding and even an appreciation of the contributions of the medieval thinkers.

Whether one thinks it is good or unfortunate, the story of Western culture is interwoven with the history of Christianity. Furthermore, Christianity as a historical force, an institution, and a system of thought would not have been what it has been apart from the way it evolved during the Middle Ages. Both the Roman Catholic and the Protestant traditions have been influenced by the great thinkers of this period. But the history of religion aside, the Middle Ages are rich with contributions that even secular thinkers have to take into account. For example, Augustine gave us the idea that history has a pattern that can be understood, and his thought has provided the model for philosophies of history ever since. While differing radically in the details, the atheistic thought of Karl Marx could be seen as a photographic negative of Augustine's view of history. Furthermore, while the early medieval thinkers had only fragments of Greek philosophy, they did have Aristotle's writings on logic. (Much of Plato's and Aristotle's work was reintroduced into western Europe only in the latter part of the Middle Ages.) Working with what they had, medieval thinkers (contrary to popular thought) excelled in the development of the science of logic. Many of the terms that are commonplace in logic today are Latin terms, derived from the medieval thinkers' work in logic. Finally, many of the arguments of the medieval philosophers have an established place as standard landmarks within philosophy today. For example, there are many philosophers who embrace the arguments for God's existence formulated by either Anselm or Aquinas. On the other hand, some philosophers question the validity of their arguments and others both question their validity and reject their conclusions. Nevertheless, the arguments of these two medieval philosophers are still taken seriously enough that their presence is commonplace in most introductions to philosophy.

Perhaps the most interesting feature of medieval philosophy is the determined effort of these thinkers to integrate the best of (Greek) philosophy with Christian thought. It provides an interesting case study of the life of ideas. It shows us how ideas survive their inventors, how different ideas repel or attract each other, how they take root in new soil, and how they become elements in new compounds created by the "conceptual chemists" of this period. This case study also shows how ideas that at first seem benign can have unanticipated consequences and how ideas that at first seem dangerous can be harnessed and domesticated. Looked at superficially, the debates of the medieval philosophers and theologians can seem abstract and sterile. But beneath the surface of these debates are some interesting issues, some unforgettable characters, some important milestones in philosophy and history, as well as an interesting chapter in the human drama.

7

Cultural Context: The Development of Christian Thought

The Encounter Between Greek and Christian Thought

In the preceding chapters, we have followed the stream of ancient Greek philosophy. Now we must backtrack and pick up another stream that crosses the previous one, mingles with its waters, carries forward some of its energy, and becomes one of the most powerful forces in Western history. This second cultural-intellectual stream is that of Hebraic thought and the Christian religion, which arose out of it. The impact Christianity has made on world history is signified by the fact that the standard method of dating historical events identifies them as either B.C. or A.D. These abbreviations stand for "before Christ" and *Anno Domini* or "in the year of the Lord." The rise of Christianity is an important turning point in the story of philosophy, for it overlapped with the decline of the Roman Empire and of Greco-Roman or Hellenistic philosophy. From very tenuous beginnings, it went on to dominate the intellectual life of Western Europe.

Initially, there were many differences between the Greek tradition and Judeo-Christian thought.

The Greeks tended to be polytheists, whereas the Jews and the Christians believed in one, supreme God. The gods of the Greeks were limited. On most accounts, they were subject to Fate. Typically, the deities in these philosophical systems were not sovereign over the world. Plato's creator (the Demiurge) had to consult the pre-existing Forms when imposing order on a pre-existing matter. Aristotle's deity was not transcendent but was immanent in the world. In contrast, the God of the Judeo-Christian tradition is all-powerful and transcendent. He created the world out of nothing and rules over it according to his sovereign will. Furthermore, Plato's ultimate principle, the Good, was impersonal, as was Aristotle's Unmoved Mover. The God of the Bible, however, was personal and had a loving concern for his creation.

Christianity presented itself as a revealed religion. Building on their Hebraic roots, the Christians claimed that God had spoken and revealed himself to us through the Old Testament prophets, in the person of Jesus of Nazareth, and in the Gospels and Epistles of the New Testament. Whereas the Greeks sought for truth and ultimate reality, the Christian message was that truth and ultimate reality (in the person of God) was searching for us. The ancient Greeks talked of the Logos, the principle of order and reason that permeates the universe. Capitalizing on this tradition, John began his Gospel by proclaiming that the Logos was identical to God and that in Jesus the Logos took on human form and dwelled among us. For Christian thinkers, human history was to be understood in terms of the themes of sin, grace, salvation, and eternal life. However, these were not viewed as a series of philosophical doctrines but as moments in the individual's spiritual journey. Although many Christian intellectuals tried to show that their faith could hold its own with the best of Greek philosophy, they did not share the Greeks' confidence that philosophical reason alone could solve the deep problems of human life.

The first-century Christians faced four immediate concerns that left little time or energy for philosophical speculation. First, they had to prepare for the second coming of Jesus. Jesus' disciples and the Apostle Paul both had the impression that Jesus would return to earth in their lifetime.[1] Since time was short and nothing earthly was of lasting value, there was no point in engaging in long-term intellectual projects. Second, the early Church had to survive persecution. For the Romans, religion was a concern of the state. Only if all its citizens made sacrifices to the gods of the state would the country prosper. Besides refusing to pay homage to the pagan gods, the Christians proclaimed that Christ, not the emperor, was lord over all the earth. Hence, to be a Christian in the Roman Empire was treasonous and a capital crime. Although the intensity of the persecution rose and fell with each different emperor, it did not completely end until the reign of Constantine the Great, the first Christian emperor, who ruled from A.D. 305 to 337.

Third, the Christians felt an urgent need to evangelize the world and spread the good news. Their goal was not to promote a set of theoretical ideas but to save people's souls by reconciling them to God. Initially, this diminished their interest in theoretical speculation. The fourth immediate concern was to fight the heresies that abounded at this time. There were many alternative versions of Christian teaching, each claiming to be the authentic version of Christian truth. Some of these were really Greek religious philosophies that were given a Christian veneer, others were simply alternative interpretations of the New Testament theology. The result was a massive confusion that threatened to drag the new religion down with the weight of controversy.

Despite these four urgent problems, Christians gradually found that they could not ignore philosophy. After several generations passed, it became increasingly clear that Jesus' return to earth was not imminent. Hence, Christians began to turn to longer-term tasks such as Christianizing their culture. The most significant development was that Christianity broadened out from its Jewish background. This shifted the focus from trying to reconcile the new faith with the Jewish tradition, to trying to reconcile the faith with the Greek tradition. By the end of the second century, Christianity had penetrated the upper classes and began to attract intellectuals in the Roman Empire. The minds of many of these educated converts had been nurtured in the soil of Greek philosophy. Hence, Christian thinkers had to come to terms with Greek ways of thinking by formulating their doctrines in the categories of Greek philosophy and by showing that their faith was intellectually respectable. For these reasons, the original task of evangelization came to be supplemented by that of apologetics. "Apologetics" is a term derived from Athenian legal procedures. It refers to the art of making a reply or providing a defense of one's position. Because Christianity was "on trial" before the court of Greek culture and philosophy, Christian thinkers sought to make the best case possible for it, using the weapons of philosophy itself. Similarly, since many of the heresies arose out of philosophy, Christian thinkers discovered they needed to "fight fire with fire." Hence, the task of rebutting false doctrines required both logical arguments and a greater clarification of the true teachings. Accordingly, Christian thinkers used the tools of Greek philosophy to support their position and to achieve conceptual precision.

The Problem of Faith and Reason

One of the first problems that Christian thinkers had to face was the relationship between faith and reason. This issue was a major concern in the early centuries of the Church, continued to be debated during the medieval period, and remains a source of lively discussion among philosophers of religion in the twentieth century. The problem was virtually without precedent in the history of philosophy up to this point. For the Greeks there was no problem. They had only one principle to guide their thinking: philosophical reason. The Greeks did not have any divine revelation in the form of sacred scriptures, for most of their religious notions were transmitted through their poets and tradition. However, the philosophers either rejected these traditions or downplayed their importance. What little they did retain from popular religion they made conform to the dictates of their philosophical systems. Likewise, the Jewish tradition had no problem with faith and reason. The Jews also avoided the problem by adhering to only one side of the dichotomy, but in their case it was faith. Their communal stories of God's faithfulness to his people made philosophical grounds for belief seem superfluous.

As Greek ways of thinking began to displace the Jewish influences on Christianity, Christian thinkers found themselves having to answer attacks from philosophers without, resolve controversies within, and satisfy the Greek thirst for a systematic worldview. The problem was that they were presented with two sources of information—revelation and philosophical reason. This situation raised several questions: Is Christian belief rational? What is the relationship between faith and reason? Can one coherently embrace both routes to the truth? If faith and reason lead to conflicting conclusions, how do we resolve the quarrel between them? Should a person of faith dabble in the speculations of pagan philosophers in the first place?

The problem was intensified by the fact that the philosophical tradition provided mixed data. The Christians found much in Greek philosophy repugnant. In addition to their differing conceptions of the nature of deity, noted earlier, a number of other problems arose. For Plato, individuals find their fulfillment not in relating to a divine creator but through exercising their autonomous reason. Plato also believed in reincarnation, a doctrine incompatible with the biblical account of the afterlife. As for Aristotle, his system did not allow for any notion of individual immortality. And the Epicureans taught that the pursuit of pleasure and not obedience to God was the goal of life. In death, according to Epicurus, the soul disintegrates with the body and there is no afterlife. Yet Christians found much to admire in Greek philosophy. Socrates and Plato did believe that the soul was an immortal, spiritual entity identical with the real person and that eternal, spiritual realities were more important than the transitory, physical world. Aristotle helpfully provided arguments for the existence of God and stressed that there was a built-in purpose to everything. The Stoics saw the cosmos as full of order, harmony, benevolence, and beauty that was directed toward the fulfillment of a divine purpose. For them, adjusting one's life to the will of God was the key to the good life.

Similarly, the biblical tradition provided mixed data. On the negative side, the Apostle Paul's first letter to the Corinthians proclaims that the wisdom of the world is foolishness in the eyes of God and that the gospel of Christ appeared foolish to the pagan world. Furthermore, Paul warned, "Make sure that no one traps you and deprives you of your freedom by some secondhand, empty, rational philosophy based on the principles of this world instead of on Christ."[2] But despite these negative points, the biblical tradition also provided a number of bridges to Greek thought. When Paul spoke to a group of Epicureans and Stoics, he said that he was providing fuller knowledge of the same God that they were already worshiping. He even went so far as to quote Stoic writers to support his theology.[3] Paul also said that even though the Greeks did not have biblical revelation, they still knew about God through his creation and had the moral law "engraved on their hearts."[4]* Furthermore, the Book of Proverbs sings praises to Wisdom in a way that even Socrates would approve. Finally, the prologue to the Gospel of John speaks of the Divine Logos and thus provided a conceptual link with Heraclitus and the Stoics. Given this mixed data, the future of Greek philosophy within the Christian tradition hung on whether or not the differences or the similarities between the two systems would be emphasized. A brief look at three Christian thinkers—Justin, Clement, and Tertullian—will provide a glimpse of how these issues were addressed.

JUSTIN MARTYR

Justin was born in Samaria around A.D. 100 to pagan parents. A passionate intellectual, he journeyed throughout the Middle East and Italy searching for a truth to embrace. He tells us that he enthusiastically tried Stoicism, Aristotelianism, and Pythagoreanism in turn, but these disappointed him and left him unsatisfied. Finally, he was attracted to Platonism, which made a lifelong impact on him. However, on encountering Christianity he found that even Platonic philosophy, the spiritual highpoint of Greek thought, fell short of what the gospel of Christ had to offer. Impressed by the consistency and courage of the Christians in the face of death, he became a convert and an articulate defender of the new religion. He suffered a martyr's death in Rome around A.D. 165, along with his associates.

Justin was cheerfully optimistic about the harmony between Christianity and Greek philosophy. To those wary of philosophy he says that the best of philosophy is "the greatest possession, and most honorable before God, to whom it leads us and alone commends us; and these are truly holy men who have bestowed attention on philosophy."[5] To

Christianity's intellectual critics he asserts that the Christian gospel and the best in pagan philosophy do not compete, but point to the same truth:

> If, therefore, on some points we teach the same things as the poets and philosophers whom you honour, and on other points are fuller and more divine in our teaching, and if we alone afford proof of what we assert, why are we unjustly hated more than all others?[6]

Justin illustrates his claim by pointing out that Plato and the Scriptures agree that our souls have a special affinity to God, that we are morally responsible for our actions, and that there is a time of reckoning in the world to come. Furthermore, Justin claims that the Good in Plato's *Republic* is clearly the same as the God of the Bible. Working from historically spurious information, Justin assumes that Socrates and Plato had so much of the truth because they were acquainted with the Pentateuch (the first five books of the Old Testament). But in addition to this, John's Gospel tells us that the Logos (Christ) gives light to all humankind. That is why, Justin says, both the Greeks and non-Greeks were able to discover fragments of God's truth apart from the Bible, because they possessed "seeds" of the Divine Reason (the "Spermatic Logos"). Accordingly, Justin says Socrates and Plato, along with Abraham, were "Christians before Christ," because they followed the Divine Reason within them. In this way, both Greek philosophy and the Old Testament were preparatory phases that found their culmination in Christianity. Educated people need not choose between Christianity or their intellectual heritage, because all truth is God's revealed truth whether it comes through the mouth of the prophets or is implanted in pagan philosophers by the Divine Logos.

CLEMENT OF ALEXANDRIA

Born of pagan parents around A.D. 150, Clement became a Christian through the influence of his teacher Pantaenus, a converted Stoic. Clement had a very broad-minded ecumenical spirit in his approach to Greek philosophy. He seemed to be quite familiar with the ancient texts in the history

*Christian philosophers such as Thomas Aquinas later justified their attempts to prove the existence of God by appealing to Paul's remarks in this passage. Also, Christian Platonists such as Augustine cited the statement that there are truths written in the human heart.

of philosophy and quotes them abundantly in support of his points. In his work *The Stromata*, he makes an impassioned argument for Christians to respect the treasures of Greek thought. Quoting Psalms 29:3, "The Lord is on many waters," Clement speculates that this includes the waters of Greek philosophy and not just those of the biblical tradition.[7] Arguing this point, he states that all truth is *one* and all wisdom is from the Lord. If we find words of wisdom in Plato, then this is from God no less than the words of the prophets. Hence, fragments of God's eternal truth have found their way even into pagan philosophy.[8] Clement is saying, in so many words, that it is foolish for Christians to reinvent the wheel. If Plato has good arguments for the immortality of the soul, then we can use his work and don't need to duplicate his efforts. Clement sees philosophy as a gift of divine providence and compares the Old Testament law with philosophy. The first was given to the Jews and the second to the Greeks, and God used both sources of wisdom to prepare hearts and minds for receiving the message of Jesus.[9]

Philosophy, Clement says, can even be a helpful tool for understanding Scripture.[10] Philosophy teaches us the skills of logic, the value of clear definitions, the analysis of language, and the ability to formulate demonstrations, all of which will lead us to truth. To diminish the impact of Paul's warning against "empty, rational philosophy," Clement emphasizes Paul's qualification that he is referring to philosophies that are "based on the principles of this world instead of Christ." Clement concludes, then, that Paul was not branding all philosophy as alien to Christianity, but only those schools such as Epicureanism that abolished providence and deified pleasure.[11]

Despite his claims that Greek philosophy is a kind of divine revelation, Clement does make some negative comments about it. As with many of the early Christian writers, he believes the Greeks stole many ethical and theological ideas from the Hebrews.[12] Furthermore, he always insists that Greek philosophy gave us only fragmentary and partial truths, whereas the Christian revelation gives us the fuller picture. Finally, too much attention to philosophy can entangle us in irrelevant quarrels:

> But those who give their mind to the unnecessary and superfluous points of philosophy, and addict themselves to wrangling sophisms alone, abandon what is necessary and most essential, pursuing plainly the shadows of words.[13]

However, philosophy pursued for its own sake can be enjoyable and profitable for the Christian, but only if we see it as a dessert that tops off the main meal.[14] Despite some of these negative comments, the portions of Clement's position that had the most lasting influence can be summed up in these words of his:

> Philosophy is not, then, the product of vice, since it makes men virtuous; it follows, then, that it is the work of God, whose work it is solely to do good. And all things given by God are given and received well.[15]

TERTULLIAN

Not all Christians were as optimistic about the possibility or desirability of a philosophically informed Christian faith. The most famous example of the negative position was a writer by the name of Tertullian. He was born around A.D. 160 to pagan parents in the North African city of Carthage. In the midst of a successful career as a trial lawyer in Rome, he became a Christian convert in 193, when he was moved by the courage of Christians who were being put to death for their faith. Tertullian's passionate personality and his polemical courtroom style shine throughout all of his writings. One recent historian has described Tertullian as

> brilliant, exasperating, sarcastic, and intolerant, yet intensely vigorous and incisive in argument, delighting in logical tricks and with an advocate's love of a clever sophistry if it will make the adversary look foolish, but a powerful writer of splendid, torrential prose.[16]

Whereas Justin and Clement delight in the Christian truths they find in the Greeks, Tertullian only grudgingly admits that sometimes philosophers found the truth. For example, he points out that the philosophers agree with the Christians that the Logos, the divine Word and Reason, created the universe.[17] However, while philosophers became inflated with pride in their own reason, their truths are not the result of spiritual insight but rather of dumb luck, much like a sailor happening to find his way in a storm:

> Of course we shall not deny that philosophers have sometimes thought the same things as ourselves. . . . It sometimes happens even in a storm, when the boundaries of sky and sea are lost in confusion, that some harbour is stumbled on (by the labouring ship) by some happy chance; and sometimes in the very shades of night, through blind luck alone, one finds access to a spot, or egress from it.[18]

On the whole, however, he has little use for philosophy. Christ tells us, "Seek and ye shall find." However, rather than this sanctioning the sort of seeking that characterizes philosophy, it tells us that when we have found the truth (the Gospel of Christ) "nothing else is to be believed, and therefore nothing else is to be sought."[19] He is troubled by the way that heresies arise out of philosophy and lumps them both with the worst of company: "It has also been a subject of remark, how extremely frequent is the intercourse which heretics hold with magicians, with mountebanks [quacks], with astrologers, with philosophers; and the reason is, that they are men who devote themselves to curious questions."[20] Tertullian describes the Apostle Paul's meeting with philosophers in Athens as an encounter with "huckstering wiseacres."[21] He also has great iconoclastic fun ridiculing the revered figure of Socrates and the philosopher's famous deathbed scene.[22]

Finally, Tertullian's most famous dismissal of the project that Justin and Clement called for is the following passage:

> What indeed has Athens to do with Jerusalem? What concord is there between heretics and Christians? . . . Away with all attempts to produce a mottled Christianity of Stoic, Platonic, and dialectic composition! We want no curious disputation after possessing Christ Jesus, no inquisition after enjoying the gospel! With our faith, we desire no further belief. For this is our [victorious] faith, that there is nothing which we ought to believe besides.[23]

In other words, just as Athens (the intellectual center of philosophy) and Jerusalem (the spiritual home of Christianity) are separated by hundreds of miles geographically, so pagan philosophy and the Christian Gospel are miles apart spiritually and can never meet.

Nothing is known of Tertullian after the date of his last literary work in the year 220. Nevertheless, he has made his place in history as the most forceful religious veto to the project of reconciling faith and philosophy. To be charitable, we can try to understand his concern with the way that alien philosophical ideologies were muddying the waters of Christian theology. Nevertheless, his attempts to build a dam separating the philosophical and biblical traditions failed. We cannot underestimate the importance of writers such as Justin and Clement in arguing for the importance of Greek philosophy for Christian thought. Certainly, the shape of Western Christianity and intellectual history would have been different if the medievals had not seen the value of preserving the Greek philosophical tradition.*

Challenging Heresies and Clarifying Orthodoxy

One of the philosophical issues facing the early Church was how to express the rather poetic theology of the Hebraic tradition in terms that would be clear and acceptable to the Greek mind. The Greek tradition with its taste for fine, logical distinctions forced Christian thinkers to give more rigorous and refined definitions of their central concepts. For the early believers, it was enough to say that God was in Christ reconciling the world to himself and that Jesus was filled with the Spirit of God. But questions arose concerning exactly what was being said in the previous sentence and

---

*There is still controversy today over the extent to which philosophical categories introduced distortions into Christian theology.

what was not being said. It did not help matters that the culture presented a spectrum of religious philosophies each vying for influence within the Church. Orthodoxy (which literally means "right belief") had to be separated from dangerous or false opinions. The Greek word *heresy* originally meant "choice" or "opinion." However, it now came to mean "incorrect opinion." Four main positions were condemned as heresies: Gnosticism, Manichaeaism, Arianism, and Pelagianism.

GNOSTICISM

The Gnostics consisted of a dozen or more sects in the second century that developed an interpretation of the new religion in which they substituted knowledge (*gnosis*) for faith. The Gnostics considered themselves superior to the rabble (including ordinary Christians) because they had an esoteric and secret body of knowledge that was revealed only to them. Gnosticism was a bizarre blend of Babylonian astrology, Egyptian cults, Persian religion, Greek mystery cults, Neo-Pythagoreanism, Neoplatonism, and Stoicism, mixed with Jewish and Christian doctrines. Actually, Gnostic sects were around long before the birth of Christianity, but it is their mingling with Christian thought that interests us here.

The Gnostics taught a pseudo-Christian mythology in which multiple deities, angels, archangels, and other spiritual beings emanated and descended from the one, supreme God. They viewed reality in terms of an extreme dualism between spirit and matter. They considered the God of the Old Testament to be an evil God who arose to become the rival of the God of Light. This dark force was called the Demiurge and was thought to have created the kingdom of evil and darkness that was identical to the world of matter. The Demiurge created the human race in an attempt to capture portions of the good, divine spirit within the physical prison of the body.

Christ was one of the highest spirits. He foiled the scheme of the Demiurge by entering into a human body (some say he merely took on the appearance of being physical). Only the spiritual elite who could comprehend the secret doctrines could escape their bondage to the material world and return to the Kingdom of Light. Because the physical world was considered evil, most of the Gnostics preached asceticism (a style of life that denies the value of anything in the physical world). A few sects, however, consisted of wanton libertines. They believed that the spirit and the body were so separate that anything that happened to the body (such as sexual promiscuity) could not affect the spirit. Some even believed that satiating physical desires would destroy their hold over people, and thus the spirit would triumph over the designs of the Demiurge.

THE MANICHAEAN HERESY

Manichaeism was founded by a third-century Iranian prophet named Mani. It could be considered an offshoot of Gnosticism because the two systems have much in common. The major difference is that the Gnostics believed that evil came into being from one of the emanations of the supreme deity, whereas the Manichaeans believed that the God of Light and the God of Darkness had existed as rivals from all eternity. Thus, they taught an extreme metaphysical dualism in which two equal but opposite forces continually struggled for dominance. One appeal of their teachings was that they did not have to explain how evil originated in a universe ruled by an all-powerful and all-good God. Their answer was that the good God was simply limited in his powers. Like the Gnostics, they believed matter was evil, created by the forces of darkness to imprison human souls. Hence, salvation was to be found by rising above involvement with the physical world through an ascetic denial of such things as meat, wine, marriage, and property. The Manichaeans sought to synthesize all religions by claiming that Buddha was the revelation of God to India, Zoroaster the prophet for Persia, Jesus the divine prophet to the West, and Mani the prophet for the present age. Obviously, Christians objected to this denial of the uniqueness of the Christian religion. Manichaeism proved a very popular and widespread religion. Augustine was a Manichaean for thirteen years before becoming a Christian, after which he became one of the most forceful critics of Manichaeism.

In summary, the two pseudo-Christian movements of Gnosticism and Manichaeism are significant for several reasons. First, they illustrate the confusing mixture of philosophical schools and mystery religions prominent at this time. All preached some form of personal salvation. By synthesizing elements from all the religious and philosophical movements of the age, these two movements became very appealing. Second, they promoted a spiritual-physical dualism, which resulted in the depreciation of the physical world. Although Gnosticism and Manichaeism were declared heresies, some of their dualism crept into the writings of the early Church theologians. Even though Christians taught that God created the physical world and declared it was good and that Christ came to earth in a physical body, a very strong element of spiritual-physical dualism and asceticism persisted throughout the Middle Ages.

Third, the way in which these pseudo-Christian philosophers perverted Christian teachings led some theologians to be suspicious of all philosophies, and these heresies fueled the anti-intellectual wing of Christianity. Finally, the confusions caused by such heresies showed Christian intellectuals the need to pursue the conceptual clarification of Christian theology.

THE NATURE OF GOD AND THE ARIAN HERESY

In the fourth century, a crisis within the Church forced Christian theologians to further clarify their doctrines. Christians proclaimed there was one God at the same time that they talked of three, equally divine persons (the Father, Son, and the Holy Spirit). The Son was identified with Jesus of Nazareth. The Son was also called the Logos, using terminology found in both the New Testament and Neoplatonism, and entailing all the latter's complications concerning the relationship of God to the Logos. From the very beginning, the problem posed by trinitarian theology was to understand how there could be both one God and three divine persons. Several extreme answers emerged to solve this riddle. On the one hand, some said that these were simply different manifestations of the one divinity, much as "the husband of Martha Washington" and "the first President of the United States" both designate George Washington. This collapsed the distinction between Jesus and the Father and seemed to imply that God the Father died on the cross. Another answer was that the three persons are related to the divine substance, the same way three distinct human persons all partake of the essence of human nature. However, this implied a sort of polytheism and contradicted the biblical tradition that there is only one God. Some solved the tension by denying that Jesus was divine at all. Others denied that he was human. In the attempt to relate three persons and one God, every logical permutation was advocated.

The controversy came to a head in the opposition of two major factions. Athanasius, who later became Bishop of Alexandria, led a party that asserted God manifested himself in three persons who shared the same divine substance. Thus the Son was of the same substance as the Father. His opponent Arius, a well-educated Alexandrian cleric, took the parental metaphor literally and claimed that the Son was created by the Father and that the two were not the same. Facing civil disorder, the Christian Emperor Constantine tried to resolve the controversy by calling a general council of bishops to meet in Nicea in 325 to settle the matter once and for all. The two spokesmen presented their cases, but the party Athanasius led was in the majority and his position prevailed, becoming the official orthodoxy, while the Arians were formally denounced and declared heretics. These proceedings produced the famous Nicene Creed (a version of which people still recite in many churches today as the official statement of Christian belief).

This did not end the matter, however. The controversy raged on for several centuries as emperors of various theological persuasions lent their support to one side or the other. The radical Arians claimed that the Son's essence is unlike (*anomoios*, in Greek) the Father's, while the Nicene formula insisted that the two were of the same being (*homoousios*). Eventually, the supporters of the Nicene Creed and their more moderate opponents found they could compromise by agreeing that the Son and the Father were of "similar substance" (*homoiousios*). This issue may seem rather abstruse, because the difference between the various positions was often very subtle and their terminology differed by a matter of only a few letters. However, these thinkers felt the purity of the faith, the divine truth, and even one's salvation were at stake on this issue. When argument failed, riots and bloodshed took its place. More debates arose over the similar question of how Christ could be both human and divine and how these two natures combined in one individual. The conflict over Arianism continued for over fifty years, and it took several Church councils to settle the issues once and for all. Even when the official position was clarified, orthodoxy had to walk a narrow tightrope to keep from falling into one heresy or another.

The philosophical significance of these issues is that they illustrate the impact of Greek philosophy on Christian thought. The Nicene Creed answers the Arian controversy by stating that Christ was "begotten, not made, being of one substance with the Father." Notice that the philosophical category of "substance" occurs in this formula. The term is never used this way in the New Testament to refer to what Christ shares with the Father. Instead, it is being used in the technical sense familiar to Greek metaphysics. In this way, Greek philosophical distinctions played a large role in defining theological problems and in setting out opposing positions. Similarly, Platonic concerns about how particulars "participate" in universals lurked behind debates over whether and how Jesus participated in the divinity of the Father. This Greek philosophical background forced Christian theologians to face these issues in a particular way. We can only speculate whether and how these issues would have been addressed if Christianity had developed in a different cultural context.

THE PROBLEM OF FREE WILL AND SIN: THE PELAGIAN HERESY

The next major controversy was provoked by a British monk named Pelagius, who settled in Rome in the early years of the fifth century. He became concerned about the doctrine of original sin. According to this teaching, when Adam (the first man) disobeyed God, the result was that sin entered into the human race. Consequently, everybody since then has inherited a sinful nature and is a slave to sin. For this reason, it is said, Christ had to come and save us from our helplessness and bondage to sin. However, God is sovereign and only extends his grace or help to those whom he will. The rest remain victims (willingly, perhaps) of their own, corrupt natures. However, Pelagius believed that this teaching led to moral apathy. If, through no fault of my own, I am born with a sinful nature and cannot resist sinning, then why should I try to avoid the unavoidable? To Pelagius, this sort of thinking pulls the rug out from underneath any notion of moral responsibility and makes the struggle to be good apparently useless. In contrast, he sincerely believed that the correct Christian position was to assert human moral freedom. He insisted that we can resist sin and make correct moral choices without outside help. That sinfulness seems the norm for humanity is because Adam cursed his race with a bad example that was passed down to each succeeding generation. So where does God fit into the Pelagian picture? The answer is that God sent Jesus to live a life of perfect love. His teachings and example help us decide to will the good. However, with or without his work in our lives, our capacity for freedom remains the same. Augustine made Pelagianism one of his targets, and this controversy helped shape much of Augustine's theology and, thereby, much theology for centuries to come. The Church eventually condemned Pelagianism as a heresy because it overemphasized human moral autonomy and tended to make divine grace and Christ's redemptive death superfluous. Yet although Pelagianism was officially put to rest, religious philosophers still wrestle with the problem of reconciling God's sovereignty with human freedom. Furthermore, the problem of how to balance the determinants on human behavior with moral responsibility continue to vex religious and secular philosophers alike.

The Future Agenda: A Christian Philosophical Synthesis

As we have seen, most of what could be called Christian philosophy during the first few centuries had a negative agenda. Christian thinkers were trying to defend their faith from philosophical attacks and were trying to straighten out the confusions of theological heresies. As Christian thought began to seep into the culture and become more secure, the more positive task of working out a Christian philosophical worldview became the next stage in the development of Christian thought. What was needed was a comprehensive view of the world and human life as seen by the light of Christian truth. In addition to tackling the core philosophical questions in epistemology, metaphysics, and ethics, Christian thinkers in the centuries to come developed philosophical perspectives on physical nature, the state, law, history, art, and psychology.

Because of its Hebraic roots, Christianity did not originally have anything that a Greek or Roman would recognize as a well-articulated philosophy. Hence, it became necessary for Christian thinkers to borrow the philosophical tools and weapons of the pagans. (Augustine compared this to the Israelites stealing the goods of the Egyptians as they left for the promised land.) Christians naturally turned to the most spiritual-minded of the Greek philosophies for their resources. Accordingly, Christian thinkers in the Middle Ages drew primarily on Platonism and Neoplatonism, along with elements borrowed from the Stoics for the foundations of their thought. However, in the latter part of the medieval period, Aristotelian philosophy emerged as another important resource for Christian thought. The chapters covering Augustine to Aquinas will examine these attempts to fulfill the Greek philosophical agenda within a Christian context.

Questions for Understanding

1. In what ways did Greek thought differ from Christian thought?

2. What were four factors that delayed the growth of philosophical thought among the early Christians?

3. Why did many first- and second-century Christian thinkers find that philosophy was unavoidable?

4. What is the problem of faith and reason? How did this problem arise in Christian thought?

5. Why did Justin Martyr believe that there could be harmony between Christianity and Greek philosophy?

6. What was Clement of Alexandria's view of the relationship between faith and reason?

7. Why did Tertullian have such a dim view of philosophy?

8. Why were the following movements condemned as heresies? Gnosticism, Manichaeaism, Arianism, and Pelagianism.

Questions for Reflection

1. Using Justin Martyr and Clement of Alexandria as your models, imagine how you would explain to someone why a person of religious faith should study philosophy.

2. Imagine that Tertullian's view of philosophy had prevailed in Western Christendom. What would be the effects of this?

3. Suppose that you were either a medieval (a) Christian, (b) Muslim, or (c) Jew. Which Greek philosophers would you find to be most helpful in developing a philosophy consistent with your faith? Why?

Notes

1. Mark 13:24–30, 1 Thessalonians 4:16–17.

2. Colossians 2:8 (The Jerusalem Bible).

3. Acts 17:28.

4. Romans 1:19–20, 2:14–15.

5. Justin Martyr, *Dialogue with Trypho*, chap. 2, in *The Ante-Nicene Fathers*, vol. 1, ed. Alexander Roberts and James Donaldson (reprint ed., Grand Rapids, MI: Eerdmans, 1956), 195.

6. Justin Martyr, *Apology I*, in Roberts and Donaldson, 169.

7. Clement of Alexandria, *The Stromata*, bk. 6, chap. 8, in *The Ante-Nicene Fathers*, vol. 2, ed. Alexander Roberts and James Donaldson (reprint ed., Grand Rapids, MI: Eerdmans, 1962), 495. Subsequent references list the book and chapter numbers followed by the page number of this edition.

8. Ibid., 1:13, 313.

9. Ibid., 1:5, 305.

10. Ibid., 1:9, 309–310.

11. Ibid., 1:11, 311.

12. Ibid., 2:18, 365; 5:14, 465.

13. Ibid., 6:18, 518.

14. Ibid.

15. Ibid., 6:17, 517.

16. Henry Chadwick, *The Early Church* (Harmondsworth, England: Penguin, 1967), 91.

17. Tertullian, *The Apology*, chap. 21, in *The Ante-Nicene Fathers*, vol. 3, ed. Alexander Roberts and James Donaldson (reprint ed., Grand Rapids, MI: Eerdmans, 1956), 34. Subsequent references to Tertullian's works cite the chapter of the original work and the page number of this edition.

18. Tertullian, *A Treatise on the Soul*, chap. 2, 182.

19. Tertullian, *On Prescription Against Heretics*, chap. 9, 247–248.

20. Ibid., chap. 43, 264.

21. Tertullian, *A Treatise on the Soul*, chap. 3, 183.

22. Ibid., chap. 1, 181–182.

23. Tertullian, *On Prescription Against Heretics*, chap. 7, 246.

8

St. Augustine:
Philosophy in the Service of Faith

AURELIUS AUGUSTINE IS ONE OF THE MOST influential writers in the history of the Christian Church. He stood at one of the major crossroads in history, the transition from the Hellenistic period to the Middle Ages. Understanding his thought is essential to understanding the Middle Ages, for he influenced medieval thought for a thousand years. He was a prolific writer, producing 118 treatises on various theological topics. However, he is important not only because he had a great impact on theology and philosophy, but also because two of his major works have made him an important figure in the history of literature. Many consider his *Confessions* the greatest spiritual autobiography of all time. The personal voice in Augustine's writings stands out in a time when most works were commentaries and objective, detached treatises. His *City of God* is noted for being the first philosophy of history. Its style is equally innovative, for he does not merely provide a description of historical events but uses them to tell a story. However, after Augustine people paid little attention to the problem of history until the eighteenth century. At this time, the intellectuals of the French Enlightenment used historical narratives to support their faith in secular progress. Working from a more theistic perspective, Giambattista Vico (1668–1744), an Italian philosopher, social theorist, and devout Catholic, made history the central theme of his philosophy. In the nineteenth century, the philosophy of history occupied the center stage in the works of such figures as Hegel, Comte, Marx, and Nietzsche.

Augustine's Life: From Passionate Pleasure to a Passionate Faith

Augustine was born in A.D. 354 in North Africa. His father, Patricius, was not a Christian (although he became one on his deathbed). However, Monica, Augustine's mother, was a devout Christian who was later declared a saint. He was a bright student and excelled in the study of the Latin classics. Seeking the best possible education for him, his parents sent him to Carthage in 370 to study rhetoric. Carthage was the most prominent city in North Africa at this time, and must have been overwhelming for a young man of sixteen. Not only was it the center of government, but it also offered all the distractions, entertainments, and vices often associated with a port city. While there, he lived with a mistress for ten years and fathered an illegitimate son by her.

Always seeking spiritual and intellectual fulfillment, Augustine fell under the influence of the Manichaean religious cult. He was impressed by their rational presentation of truth, for they seemed to have the only reasonable answer as to why there is evil in the world, if a good God exists. As we saw in the previous chapter, the Manichaeans believed that there are two competing powers in the world, one good and the other evil. Since these opposing powers are in an eternal struggle for supremacy, this explains why we find both good and evil in the world. Human beings are a prime example of this struggle. Our souls are that part of us that participates in the power of goodness and light. They are at war with our bodies, which are products of the evil and dark force. Besides the intellectual attractions of this view, it also gave Augustine the comfort that his true self, his soul, was essentially good and his passions and sensual desires could be blamed on an outside cause. However, these spiritual struggles did not dilute his worldly ambitions. He pursued a successful career teaching rhetoric and literature, even winning a prize for his poetry. After nine years he became disillusioned with Manichaean thought. Faustus, the master teacher of Manichaean doctrines, paid a visit to Carthage. Seeking him out for answers to his questions, Augustine was dismayed to find out that he was a pompous simpleton.

Eventually, Augustine went to Rome to further his career and to seek better students. By this time he had adopted skepticism as his philosophical outlook. In 384 he ended up in Milan as a professor of rhetoric. At the request of Augustine's mother, he was befriended by St. Ambrose, the Bishop of Milan. Although he was impressed by the bishop's Christianity, Augustine's passions were so strong that he could not bring himself to change his lifestyle. His continual struggle against his lusts is vividly illustrated by his honest prayer to God: "Grant me chastity and continence, but

St. Augustine in his study. With Plato, Augustine believed that eternal truths could be found by searching inward. However, Augustine added that reason is not a neutral instrument but is affected by the orientation of our hearts, our passions, and our spiritual openness.

not yet" (C 8.7.17).[1] Giving up on any pretentions to moral purity, he took another mistress.

He began to read the Neoplatonists, including Plotinus, in earnest. Their teachings inspired him to turn inward and to seek after spiritual reality. He says that the Platonists gave him a glimpse, as though from a mountaintop, of the homeland of peace, but it was the writings of the apostle Paul that showed him the way to it (C 7.21.27). Augustine was moved when he heard of the Christian conversion of the great teacher Victorinus, a renowned translator of the Neoplatonists and Aristotle's logic, who was honored with a statue in the Roman Forum. Augustine was amazed that a man having such a reputation for scholarship could have the courage to publicly profess his Christian faith.

In the summer of 386, Augustine's constant inner turmoil eventually led him to the point of his own conversion. He wandered out into a garden and paced around in a state of extreme agitation. Within him, a voice said, "Let it be now" (C 8.11.25). However, he also heard the voice of his lustful passions say, "Are you getting rid of us?" and he was taunted by the question, "Do you think that you can live without them?" (C 8.11.26). In a state of misery and choked with tears, Augustine read a passage from St. Paul and a sense of peace and resolution filled his heart as he yielded to God. Subsequently, he was baptized by St. Ambrose on Easter Sunday in 387. Deciding to devote all his energies to the work of the Church, he abandoned the teaching of rhetoric and returned to his home in Africa in the region now known as Tunisia. In 396 he was made Bishop of Hippo. Augustine died in 430, as the barbarians were taking over the Empire and surging at the gates of Hippo.

Augustine's Task: Understanding the Human Predicament

The content of Augustine's writings slowly evolved as his thought developed in response to the different philosophical and theological issues he faced throughout his life. His early period culminates with his autobiographical *Confessions* (finished around 400). During this period, Augustine tended to be fairly optimistic about the capabilities of reason and mainly addressed topics that can be handled by natural reason alone. His early works include refutations of the Manichaean and skeptical philosophies of his youth. His later writings, which include *City of God* (completed in 426), are more scripturally based and insist more strongly that reason is subordinate to faith. Their explicit theological content reflects both Augustine's developing interests and the threat posed by Christian heresies such as Pelagianism.

In every aspect, Augustine's philosophy draws deeply from the wells of Platonic and Neoplatonic philosophy. He is well aware of this, for he notes that "none of the other philosophers has come so close to us as the Platonists have" (CG 8.5).* Since they "have unlawful possession" of God's truth, we should not shrink from their ideas but can rightfully claim them for ourselves (CD 2.40.60). At the same time that he uses the resources of pagan philosophy, there are few thinkers whose thought was as passionately Christian as Augustine's. "God and the soul, that is what I desire to know. Nothing more? Nothing whatever" (SL 1.7). Augustine never met a purely intellectual problem. All philosophical ideas are either obstacles or vehicles in the journey of the soul to God and eternal life. For this reason, Augustine did not write rigid, systematic treatises, but used the rhetorical style that earned him fame in his first career. His philosophical energies were spent either hammering at the enemies of the faith or paving the road that would lead his audience to God.

Augustine's philosophy emphasized (particularly in his later works) that no aspect of our world can be understood apart from a religious perspective. He refuses to make the distinctions that would be important to Thomas Aquinas centuries later: natural reason versus supernatural revelation, philosophy versus theology, humans understood as natural beings versus humans as spiritual beings. Instead, Augustine insists that knowledge, philosophy, the world, and humanity are always to be understood in the light of their religious significance. Where Scripture is silent on some intellectual issue that concerns him, Augustine is content to adopt the answers of Plato found in the *Meno* and the *Timaeus* and Plotinus in the *Enneads*. These occasions are rare, however, for he thinks that the Bible gives us the final perspective on both our moral and intellectual concerns. For the most part, secular philosophies can only add a few flourishes to this.

---

*Augustine later regretted that he had been so uncritical of the Platonists. Although still retaining many of their insights, he found it necessary to modify their position.

Two central issues lie at the heart of Augustine's philosophy. These are (1) the primacy of the will and (2) the fact that love motivates all action, both human and divine. The doctrine of the primacy of the will has two dimensions, for it applies both to his view of God and humanity. First, with respect to God, everything in the universe is a result of his free and sovereign will. Second, with respect to us, everything human is to be explained on the basis of the will. Hence, unlike the Greeks, Augustine did not believe that reason is primary. According to him, the intellect follows the will, not the other way around. But what determines the will? Augustine's answer is that nothing does; the will is completely free. At this point, the theme of love joins the first one. The will is moved in the direction of what it chooses to love. Like a physical object that is pulled by its weight toward the center of the earth, so every one of us is pulled by the affections of our hearts toward that which is the center of our lives. As Augustine says, "My weight is my love. Wherever I am carried, my love is carrying me" (C 8.9).

The problem we face, according to Augustine, is that ever since the disobedience of the first man and woman, Adam and Eve, the human race has fallen into the downward spiral of sin. The result of this original sin, which every one of us inherits and re-enacts in our own lives, is that every area of human life has been infected and corrupted by sin. Our wills are bent away from God, and the weight of our love is pulled in the wrong direction. We tend toward self-love and love of a corrupt and passing world, both of which prevent us from finding true fulfillment. Augustine tries to convince us that this human predicament affects not only our ethical life but our quest for knowledge and the entire course of human history. In fact, because the human moral predicament permeates all of Augustine's thought, I will not devote a separate section to his ethics. The preceding points lead to one of the major tensions in Augustine's philosophy, which is how to reconcile the total power of God and the effects of our sinful nature on the one hand, with his claim that humans have free will.

Theory of Knowledge: The Truth Is Within

Although Augustine says a great deal about the nature of knowledge, he was not interested in it as an end in itself. Neither was he interested in knowledge for the sake of controlling the physical world. For Augustine, epistemology serves a practical, religious purpose. It weeds out false views of knowledge that subvert the soul's journey to God, and it guides us in the search for truth. Not only is having truth a key ingredient to a happy life, but a clarified vision of truth also brings us closer to the Author of all truth.

THE QUEST FOR CERTAINTY

For the sake of these goals, Augustine was concerned with the quest for certainty. To him, nothing less than certain, eternal, and absolute truth could provide an adequate foundation for one's life. In one of his early works, *Against the Academicians*, he addresses himself to the Skeptics of the New Platonic Academy.* They maintained two theses: (1) nothing can be known, and (2) assent should not be given to anything (AA 3.10.22). Many Skeptics believed that people find wisdom and happiness in pursuing the truth rather than in actually attaining it. According to Augustine, however, someone who does not know the truth cannot be wise nor can someone be happy who never obtains what he or she strives to possess. Thus, to be wise and happy, we must find a way out of skepticism.

To defeat total skepticism, Augustine need only find some proposition P such that we are certain P is true. As a matter of fact, he finds many propositions that we know to be true. First, he points out that even the Skeptic makes truth claims. The Skeptic claims he knows his own position to be true and that it logically follows from

---

*This was the period in the Academy that was dominated by Carneades (c. 213—c. 128 B.C.). Augustine was probably familiar with the Skeptics primarily through the writings of Cicero.

premises that are true (AA 3.9.18). Here is how Augustine argues that skepticism is self-refuting:

(1) The Skeptics claim we cannot know anything to be true.

(2) To deny that we can know the truth requires a definition of truth. (Carneades uses a definition borrowed from Zeno the Stoic.)

(3) This definition is either true or false.

(4) If this definition is true, then the Skeptics know some truths. (The Skeptics refute their own claim.)

(5) If this definition is false, then it is useless in the defense of Skepticism. (The Skeptics' claim is meaningless, since they have no definition of truth.)

Next, Augustine points out that certain logical propositions are known to be true, such as "Either *P* or *Not-P* is true" and "It is false that *P* and *Not-P* are both true." Without the principles of logic, we could not reason or even articulate a position such as skepticism. For example, we know the following claim must be true: "Either the skeptics' definition is true or it is false" (AA 3.10.21). Continuing to hammer away at the Skeptics' claim that we can't have knowledge, Augustine presents mathematical truths such as "3 x 3 = 9" as truths we can know with certainty.

In the next part of his refutation, Augustine discusses the Skeptics' claim that sense experience is unreliable. His response is that what the senses report to us is always true as long as we do not go beyond the data as they are presented to us and draw unwarranted conclusions from them. For example, if I see that the oar in the water appears to be bent, this is not an illusion but is the literal truth. The oar *appears* to be bent. Augustine makes the important point here that reason needs to interpret the data of the senses before we draw any conclusions about what we really have before us (AA 3.11.26).

From his analysis of the senses, Augustine goes on to discuss yet another kind of certitude. We can be certain about the contents of our own minds as presented to us in self-conscious, inner experience. This includes the experiences we are having, our psychological and cognitive processes, and our feelings. Even our doubts create certainties. In a passage in another work that preceded Descartes's similar but more famous argument by more than twelve hundred years, Augustine argues that his own doubts lead to certainty concerning his own existence:

> For, we are, and we know that we are, and we love to be and to know that we are. . . . In the face of these truths, the quibbles of the skeptics lose their force. If they say, "What if you are mistaken?" well, if I am mistaken, I am. For, if one does not exist, he can by no means be mistaken. . . . I am most certainly not mistaken in knowing that I am. Nor, as a consequence, am I mistaken in knowing that I know. For, just as I know that I am, I also know that I know. And when I love both to be and to know, then I add to the things I know a third and equally important knowledge, the fact that I love. (CG 11.26)

It is ironic that Augustine, who laid the foundations of medieval philosophy, also developed the very point with which Descartes laid the foundations of modern philosophy. This notion is that the quest for knowledge begins with the self. To summarize what Augustine has established thus far, since we know with certainty that some propositions are true, skepticism is wrong and it is reasonable to search for further truths.

PLATONIC RATIONALISM

As with so much of his philosophy, Augustine uses typical Platonic terms and arguments to articulate his epistemology. There are some differences, however. Augustine does not devalue the senses quite as much as Plato does. After all, they were created by God along with the sensory world they deliver to us. The senses have their appropriate role to play in our practical life. Nevertheless, he agrees with Plato that the senses cannot give us eternal, perfect truth and, therefore, must be relegated to a lower level of knowledge. Hence, Augustine accepts the Platonic dualism and maintains that there are two distinct kinds of knowable objects, "those things which the mind perceives by the bodily senses; the other, of those which it perceives by itself" (HT 15.12.21). In

Augustine's view, therefore, the senses are but an instrument used by and subject to the inner person (the mind or soul). Sense experience by itself cannot give us knowledge. The mind must examine, interpret, classify, correlate, and judge the sense data. It does so by referring to nonphysical and eternal reasons that reside within.

Therefore, the highest truths are to be found in the intellect and the inner recesses of the soul. Thus Augustine advises, "Do not go outside thyself, but return to within thyself; for truth resides in the inmost part of man" (TR 39.72). In addition to Platonic reasons for this conviction, Augustine is also mindful of the biblical claim that the soul is made in the image of the God of all truth.

We now need to ask two questions: (1) What is the nature of these inward truths? and (2) How does the mind come to be aware of them? With respect to the first question, Augustine sticks very closely to Plato's theory of the Forms. For example, he refers approvingly to Plato's notion that we can recognize and judge the beauty of physical things only if the nonphysical Form of Beauty resides in the mind:

> If there is any loveliness discerned in the lineaments of the body, or beauty in the movement of music and song, it is the mind that makes this judgment. This means that there must be within the mind a superior form, one that is immaterial and independent of sound and space and time. (CG 8.6)

Similarly, in a series of arguments that would have made Plato proud, Augustine uses mathematics to argue for the existence of a higher reality that transcends the senses and the physical world. Briefly, he argues that physical realities are particular, temporal, changing, and discovered through experience. In contrast, mathematical laws and numbers are universal, eternal, unchanging, and discovered only through the intellect. Therefore, he concludes, there must be two kinds of reality (FCW 2.8).

Not surprisingly, Augustine also includes ethical norms among the higher truths that we know through a kind of "intellectual sight": "we should live justly," "the worse should be subordinate to the better," "equals should be compared with equals," and "to each should be given his own"

(FCW 2.10.113). He argues that since we all share these "true and immutable rules of wisdom," they are not human creations but are objective truths that we discover.

DIVINE ILLUMINATION

How does the mind come to know these eternal truths? Augustine answers this question with his theory of illumination. Although reason operates in a different realm from the senses, Augustine frequently uses the Platonic analogy between physical perception of the external world and our interior, mental vision. He tends to follow Plato very closely, but on some points he departs from the Platonic theory. For example, Plato believed that the mind retains knowledge from a previous existence before this life. Augustine may have originally found this view attractive, but its theological difficulties required him to reject it. Neither does he hold that these truths are simply "programmed" into us and capable of being known by our own, natural reason. Instead, he claims we discover these intelligible realities, eternal truths, forms, divine ideas (Augustine uses all these terms) through the illumination of the divine light. He did not clarify the details of this process, and scholars differ on exactly what Augustine meant to say. Nevertheless, he clearly believed that the divine light is to the mind what the sun is to the eyes (a metaphor that he borrowed from Plato). Thus, every human mind depends on God's light to see the truth.* This does not occur through a mystical, religious experience, for even the minds of the atheists are illumined, although they do not recognize the source of their light.

Even though he rejects Plato's notion of the pre-existence of the soul, Augustine still retains the metaphor of "remembering" to describe the discovery of truth. In fact, as he points out, our word *cognition* comes from the Latin *cogito*, which can mean "I recollect." Thus, the divine light can

---

*To emphasize the universality of divine illumination, Augustine refers to the prologue of the Gospel of John, which says that the true light is that which "enlightens every man who comes into the world" (CG 10.2).

illumine the truth within us, but we may fail to notice it, just as we can look at a physical object and yet not really see it. The process of apprehending the truth is like taking an algebra test and thinking that a certain type of problem is impossible, but suddenly remembering that we do know how to work it after all. In all thinking, the mind is becoming aware of, collecting, and assembling knowledge that was scattered, concealed, and neglected in remote corners of the mind (C 10.11.18).

He refers to the nonsensory contents of the mind as *memoria* (C 10.8.15). Although this includes literal memories, it also includes everything present to the mind, even if only dimly or tacitly known. This would include knowledge of the self, the truths of reason, ethical truths, values, and God himself. When I look inward I get a glimpse of an infinite realm of truths, leading to the paradox that "I myself cannot grasp the totality of what I am" (C 10.8.15). When I explore the depths of my mind, I am astonished to find a transcendent realm revealed to me. Thus, going inward leads me to an upward journey, beyond the physical world, beyond the self, where I will find what is eternal, and finally be led to God.

FAITH AND REASON

Thus far, most of Augustine's epistemology sounds very similar to Plato's. However, a crucial difference is Augustine's claim that reason cannot function properly apart from faith. For Augustine, faith and reason are not two independent and alternative routes to the truth. First, this would eliminate the need for faith. Second, this assumes the total self-sufficiency of human reason, something Augustine refuses to grant. Third, this assumes the intellect is a purely neutral instrument that takes in data and processes it. However, far from being morally neutral, Augustine believes reason is a function of the whole person and is affected by the orientation of our hearts, our passions, and our faith. As he puts it, "Faith seeks, understanding finds; whence the prophet says, 'Unless ye believe, ye shall not understand' " (HT 15.2.2).

If Augustine is correct, reason is not a neutral calculating machine, because it cannot function independently from the rest of life. My cognitive activities and my moral nature affect one another. To put Augustine's point very bluntly, if I am cheating on my income tax, having an affair with my neighbor's spouse, and am smug and complacent about my own moral autonomy, it is unlikely I would be moved by a philosophical proof for the existence of God. To acknowledge a divine lawgiver would require submission of my will and a change in my life that I am not inclined to desire. Even though the divine light illumines every mind, how much of the divine illumination we can see depends on the condition of our heart (CD 1.9.9). If you try to point something out to me on the horizon, I see it only if my eyes are open and turned in the correct direction. Similarly, reason leads me to divine truth only if the will and the desires are properly oriented. Socrates thought that having knowledge of the good leads us to pursue it. But Augustine's own moral struggles convinced him that knowledge does not produce goodness. In fact, the reverse is true. Philosophical reason only finds the light of truth if led by a heart that cherishes the light. According to Augustine, "Faith goes before; understanding follows after" (SR 118.1).

Metaphysics: God, Creation, Freedom, and Evil

THE EXISTENCE OF GOD

Many theistic philosophers in the modern period (such as Descartes and Locke) develop their epistemology independently of theological considerations. Only then do they go on, in good logical order, to provide proofs for the existence of God. Obviously, this was not the case with Augustine, for the light of faith illumines all his philosophical discussions. Nevertheless, he does offer what we may view as arguments for the existence of God. One does not get the impression he intends them to be conclusive proofs that will cause hard-boiled atheists to fall to their knees. They are more like clues or reminders that help people with open hearts find what they seek.

Although he does not believe the finite can ever prove the infinite, Augustine does believe creation gives us evidence of its Creator:

The very order, changes, and movements in the universe, the very beauty of form in all that is visible, proclaim, however silently, both that the world was created and also that its Creator could be none other than God. (CG 11.4)

Such passages are as much of an argument for God's existence from nature as can be found in Augustine. He thought, no doubt, that sense experience is too uncertain and the physical world it represents is too changeable and unlike the Creator to be an effective basis for belief.

Augustine expends much more ink arguing from the nature of the person to God's existence. He believes God is actually closer to us than the world he has made. The spiritual, inner person, made in the image of God, brings us much closer to what we are seeking than does the physical world. The quest for God leads "from the exterior to the interior, and from the interior to the superior."[2] Augustine's typical approach can be found in *On Free Choice of the Will*, where, as mentioned, he argues for the objective and universal nature of the eternal truths of reason such as found in mathematical and ethical judgments. Briefly, he argues that if there is eternal and necessary truth that is higher than the mind and independent of it, then this must be God, for these are attributes of God himself. Throughout his works, Augustine tends to uncritically identify Plato's Good with God. However, he ignores the fact that Plato's Good and the eternal truths were impersonal and a far cry from the full-blown Judeo-Christian God Augustine slips in at the end of his arguments.

CREATION

The familiar first line of the Bible begins by declaring, "In the beginning God created the heavens and the earth." Augustine, of course, believed this on faith, but he also thought that reason supported this claim. In discussing creation, Augustine makes five important points: (1) God created out of nothing, (2) creation was an act of divine freedom, (3) the

world is composed of form and matter, (4) biological species emerge from seminal forms, and (5) God created time itself. As much as he respected and borrowed from Platonic and Neoplatonic thought, Augustine is at pains on this topic to distinguish the Judeo-Christian picture of God's relation to the world from that of the Greeks.

First, he asserts that the world was brought into being out of nothing (*ex nihilo*). Here, he is rejecting all the options favored by the Greeks. The Greeks tended to believe that the world was either eternal or created out of some sort of pre-existing matter separate from God. But the Bible says God created the world without depending on any prior materials, and Augustine thinks reason confirms this. He imagines that the heavens and the earth cry out, "We did not make ourselves, we were made by him who abides for eternity" (C 9.10.25). The reason why they must have been created is because they exhibit change and variation (C 11.4.6). His assumption here is that anything changing is created and anything unchanging (such as the laws of mathematics and God) is eternal. Hence, the world is not eternal, and not a portion of God, either, for that would drag a part of God's being down into the domain where things change and are destroyed. With Plato, Augustine believes that a perfect being could not change, for the only thing he could change into would be a lesser form of being.

Second, Augustine insists that creation was a free act. Since God is sovereign, the world did not flow from him by necessity as Plotinus thought. He created because he wanted to share his goodness with creatures (TR 18.35–36). Third, the world of particulars is based on the eternal forms. In understanding the physical world, Augustine borrows liberally from Plato. Augustine spends an entire chapter of his *Confessions* interpreting the creation story in Genesis to fit his Platonism (C 12). Every part of creation is brought into existence as a combination of form and matter. However, in at least two ways Augustine deviates from Plato's account. One difference is that, for Augustine, the eternal forms, which are the archetypes or exemplars of physical objects, do not autonomously exist on their own, but reside within God's mind. Augustine says that "no determining form by which any mutable being is what it is . . . could have any existence apart from Him who truly exists because His existence is immutable" (CG 8.6).* The other difference is that he rejects Plato's view that the creator of the world (the Demiurge) functions like an architect who imposes the Forms on pre-existing matter. Augustine argues that such formless matter would have needed a creator to cause it to exist (C 11.5.7).

Augustine's fourth thesis about creation is that God has placed rational seeds or seminal reasons (*rationes seminales*) in the world, from which future created beings will emerge.† He introduces this thesis to resolve an apparent contradiction in Scripture. On the one hand, it speaks of God as having "created all things together."[3] On the other hand, in Genesis it appears that different kinds of creatures were created on different days.‡ Augustine's answer is that God did create everything simultaneously but some things were created fully developed and some as undeveloped "seeds." The immense variety of biological organisms that continue to emerge over time has developed from these rational seeds or forces planted in the world. In proposing this account, Augustine is trying to ensure that nothing is left to purely natural forces or the agency of creatures, for God is the cause of everything. Thus, even when new forms of life emerge, it is all part of God's original creation. Although it may seem that Augustine is proposing a version of theistic evolution, his account differs from the biological theory of evolution because there is no emergence of random novelties nor the transformation of one species into another, because the whole developmental scheme is there in the beginning.

Finally, Augustine considers the nature of time by pondering what the book of Genesis means when it says, "In the beginning God created. . . ." According to the Manichaeans, if the world had a beginning, then we are naturally led to ask, "What was God doing before he made heaven and earth?" Augustine rebukes those who give the following frivolous answer to this question: "He was preparing hell for those who pry into mysteries" (C 11.12). His own, more serious answer is that the question is based on the debatable assumption that time was ticking away before creation. If this were so, then why did God create at one particular time rather than sooner or later? The Manichaeans were right—if God was waiting around for eons and then, at a certain time, decided to create the world, this would imply change in God. Augustine's answer to all this is that God did not create the world *in* time, but created the world *and* time together. Since time is change, it, too, is creaturely and must have had a beginning, along with the stars, the planets, the earth, and biological species. As Augustine says, "the changes of things make time" (C 12.8.8). Time is a relational entity. Without creation, nothing would move or change and time would not pass. For God there is neither before nor after he simply is, for his existence is timeless and eternal.

FOREKNOWLEDGE, PROVIDENCE, AND FREE WILL

The previous section concluded with Augustine's view that God created time but does not exist in it, for he exists in eternity. Time is merely the way *we* experience the world. To understand God's relation to time, Augustine looks to an analogy in human experience. He notices he can hold in his mind, all at once, a particular psalm that he knows well. As he repeats it, some of the words recited become past and some are there in memory, waiting to be spoken. Thus, he can anticipate the future words to come (C 11.28.38). So it is with God. All the moments within time are known to God as one eternal present moment. Similarly, Mozart claimed that when the inspiration for a musical piece originally came to him, he did not hear

---

*Although this view can be found in the Neoplatonists, Augustine wrongly assumes that Plato also held it. The problem is that he naively assumes that Plato's Good can be equated with the biblical God.
†Augustine's notion of the rational seeds probably came to him from Plotinus but originated with the Stoics.
‡Augustine correctly realizes that the word "day" here does not necessarily mean a twenty-four-hour period, but can mean an indefinite period of time.

the notes in his mind successively, as we do when the piece is played. Instead, he could hear the whole composition in his imagination *all at once*, much as we can survey all parts of a painting in one simultaneous experience.[4] Although Mozart's instantaneous experience of a lengthy musical piece is remarkable for a human being, this is the way that God knows every temporal event.

God's foreknowledge seems to raise a problem for human freedom. If God sees ahead of time every action you will perform, then how can your actions be free? You may be wrestling with the decision of whether to go to law school after graduation or to join a business. You may have to decide whether to marry the person you are dating or to become free and unattached again. From your perspective, the outcome of these decisions are not yet decided, but Augustine says God knows what you will do. Your future life is as familiar to him as the events in a movie that you have seen many times. Since God's foreknowledge is infallible, it would seem you are suffering from the illusion of freedom. The script of your life is already contained in the mind of God. Are we forced to choose between God's foreknowledge and human freedom? Augustine doesn't think so. As he says, "God knows all things before they happen; yet, we act by choice in all those things where we feel and know that we cannot act otherwise than willingly" (CG 5.9). According to Augustine's theory, when you freely make the decision to go to law school, you were equally free not to go to law school. However, God knew beforehand that you would *freely* make the choice that you did.

Although problems enough riddle this position, Augustine aggravates them by suggesting that God not only fore*knows* what people will do, he also fore*ordains* their actions. Since God's power is supreme, Augustine thinks that human choices cannot frustrate God's will. "For He is not truly called Almighty if He cannot do whatsoever He pleases, or if the power of His almighty will is hindered by the will of any creature whatsoever" (E 96).

God's intervention in every detail of human history is dramatically illustrated by Augustine's own account of his life. He decided to leave Carthage and go to Rome to seek out better students. Or at least Augustine *thought* that was why he went to Rome. Actually, he says, God made that decision so that Augustine would be led to salvation. As he expresses this in a prayer to God, "You were using my ambitious desires as a means towards putting an end to those desires" (C 5.8). We might try to soften the conflict between human freedom and divine providence by saying that God is a superpsychologist who carries out his plans by using his knowledge of our inner motives, yet without violating our freedom. However, this does not detract from the fact that Augustine thinks that God orchestrates not only external events, but also people's actions. In Augustine's life, God made the students in Carthage incorrigible and the teaching in Rome more attractive.

Augustine does not compromise when he talks about God's power. He says that "God works in the hearts of men to incline their wills whithersoever He wills, whether to good deeds according to His mercy, or to evil after their own deserts" (GFW 43). Although some argue that so much divine sovereignty negates human freedom, Augustine simply replies that the two are compatible. For example, he says faith and works are commanded, but they are also a gift of God so that "we may understand *both* that *we do them, and that God makes us* to do them" (PS 22, emphasis added). People continue to debate the plausibility of this sort of "both-and" position in this century.

THE PROBLEM OF EVIL

In repeatedly asserting God's omnipotence, Augustine raises the problem of evil. If God is all powerful and good, how can so much suffering and evil infect the world? Before he became a Christian, Augustine thought that the Manichaeans' dualism was the only way to absolve God of blame. If the God of Light is limited in power and is caught in an eternal struggle with the competing power of darkness, then no one can suppose God is responsible for the evil in creation. Of course, the notion of God having a more or less equal adversary is not acceptable to Augustine's Christian theology. Augustine's starting point on this issue is the claim that since God created the world, anything that exists is good (C 7.12.18). Therefore, evil must always be understood as a defect, a corruption, or a perversion of what was created good. Although Augustine derived his solution to the problem of evil from the Neoplatonic tradition, he rejected their tendency to view material reality as essentially evil and in necessary tension with the rational and the spiritual. With the goodness of creation as his initial premise, Augustine offers several ways of understanding the presence of evil.

First, while some things may seem evil to us, they are actually instrumental ways of achieving the good. To use a contemporary example, no one likes to see a baby cry when she receives a vaccination shot. But this actually enables her to achieve something good, namely health. Similarly, Augustine says the calamities of this life encourage us to yearn for the life to come, and not to covet material goods, thus achieving spiritual health (CG 1.8, 22.22). Like the baby, we tend to notice only the immediate problem and miss God's benevolent purpose.

Augustine's second answer is that evil is not an independent reality but is really a type of privation, a lack of something (CG 11.22). Just as a shadow is not substantial in itself but represents the absence of light, so evil is not part of the inventory of the universe but is simply the absence of perfect goodness. But nothing in creation can match the perfect goodness of God, so everything is inevitably imperfect to some degree. If God eliminated all imperfection from the world, then everything except himself would disappear. On the whole, the world is the "masterpiece of our Creator."

> If the beauty of this order fails to delight us, it is because we ourselves, by reason of our mortality, are so enmeshed in this corner of the cosmos that we fail to perceive the beauty of a total pattern in which the particular parts, which seem ugly to us, blend in so harmonious and beautiful a way. (CG 12.4)

However, Augustine acknowledges that it may take an act of faith to believe, contrary to appearances, that all things contribute to the "beauty of a total pattern."

Augustine's third answer to the problem of evil is to shift the blame to human perversity. All natural evils (such as pain, earthquakes) are only apparently evil; the only thing that approaches genuine evil is moral evil. Moral evil is the product of the human will. It too is a privation, in that it is the result of a defective will turning away from God. According to Augustine, Adam, the first man, was the only one who had the freedom not to sin. However, after Adam freely chose to disobey God, the human race lost its freedom and became a slave to sin. Thus, it is impossible for us to not sin. We achieve true moral freedom only when God gives us the gift of grace. Augustine does not believe that the will first turns to God and then receives grace. Instead, we first receive grace, which enables our will to turn to God. For his own purposes, God grants his grace to some but not to others, but this distribution is not based on merit, for then grace would be something God owed us and would be a source of pride (the root origin of all sin), not a gift that God freely bestows. But isn't it unjust for God to give grace to some and not to others? Augustine does not think so. His point can be made as follows: If ten people have borrowed money from me, they all owe me a debt. If I cancel the debt of two of them, the rest can't complain about this because it does not change the original fact that they owe me money. Canceling the debt of some is a gift I freely give, not something any debtor can claim he or she deserves.

Augustine's view of human nature raises again the question of how we can be determined yet free. If our sinful nature makes it impossible not to sin, then it seems we are not free. Yet, since the source of our actions comes within and is rooted in our character, Augustine believes this is sufficient for free will. Are we free to do otherwise than sin? In one sense we are. There are no physical restraints on us, and no logical necessity constrains us. In everything we do, we are following what we love. Who could ask for more freedom? It is just a fact of our condition, according to Augustine, that apart from God's grace our love is distorted.

Philosophy of History and the State

THE RISE OF A CHRISTIAN PHILOSOPHY OF HISTORY

Significantly, until this point we have not discussed the philosophy of history in reference to any previous philosophers. Augustine offers us the first speculative philosophy of history that claims to uncover the purpose and pattern of history. Many Greeks, such as Plato, were concerned only with eternal, unchanging truths, and thus the fleeting, particular events of history held little interest for them. And those who defended a materialist metaphysics thought everything was governed by blind, random forces. No matter what the details of their metaphysics, the typical Greek thought human history follows the same sort of cyclical pattern we find in the seasons. Nations come into being, rise to power, and then fade away, and this cycle is repeated endlessly. There is little more to be said, for there is no overarching purpose to it all. According to Augustine, however, this view implies that the human soul is trapped on an endless, cosmic "merry-go-round" (CG-B 12.14).

In contrast to the Greek view, the Old and the New Testaments of the Bible said that history has meaning and a linear direction. Like a carefully crafted drama, history has a beginning, a middle, and an end. Although God is the author, both he and the human actors have their respective roles to play on the stage of history. Thus, it is not by accident that the first philosopher of history was a Christian.

A concern for the pattern of history fits in with Augustine's Christian vision of the world, but his writings on this topic were provoked by a startling event. The once invincible city of Rome was attacked and ravished for three days by the Goths in 410. They depleted its riches and left corpses and ruins in their wake. Our reaction would be similar to that of the Romans if Washington, DC, were captured and looted by an invading army. This event was met with a great deal of despair throughout the Empire as people

asked, "How could the great city of Rome have fallen?" It did not take long for the answers to come. The Romans who were still pagans blamed Christianity. Rome fell to the barbarians, they said, because she turned away from the gods that had supported her throughout her days of glory. In 382 Christians had removed the Goddess of Victory from the Senate House in Rome, over the protests of the pagans. Furthermore, the Christian emperor Theodosius I had decreed that the worship of Jupiter (the chief Roman god) and Mars (the god of war) and the rest of the pagan gods was a crime punishable by death. It seemed clear to many that the Christians had robbed Rome of its divine protectors and the secret of its success. Augustine defended Christianity with *City of God*, the monumental work he considered his masterpiece. It occupied the last years of his life, for he started it at the age of fifty-nine, in the year 413, and finished at age seventy-two, in 426. It is an encyclopedic work, consisting of twenty-two books and over a thousand pages. In it, he argues that Rome's strength resulted from its civic virtues, for God honored these ideals by granting Rome temporal success. In fact, her highest moral ideals were the same virtues as those taught in Christianity. However, the Romans turned against their better side and fell into decadence and rampant vice. In short, the problem was not that Rome turned to Christianity but that it did not turn soon enough. Accordingly, Augustine spends the first half of this very large volume recounting the sins of Rome's polytheism, sexual depravity, social injustice, and obscene theater shows.* The second half of the book speaks more generally about the drama of human history. The picture he presents is one in which history is seen neither as a product of economic forces, nor political struggles, nor material resources, nor blind chance, but as a moral drama in which the purposes of God and the moral decisions of human creatures are the significant elements.

*Augustine's passages have given us a wealth of information about ancient societies and polytheism, because the sources that informed his research are now lost.

THE TWO CITIES

Augustine tells the story of history by means of his famous hypothesis that human history is an ongoing conflict between two kingdoms: the City of the World and the City of God. These two kingdoms are not actual political states. Instead, they represent diametrically opposed spiritual systems that have existed since the human race turned against God and fell from grace. However, every particular political state serves the interests of one or the other spiritual kingdom. Thus, Augustine assumes with Plato that society has the same moral structure as the individual. We are to understand societies as well as individual people in terms of their basic loves or commitments. Each of us is a citizen of one or the other of these "cities," depending on whether we love God or the world. Augustine describes the two cities:

> What we see, then, is that two societies have issued from two kinds of love. Worldly society has flowered from a selfish love which dared to despise even God, whereas the communion of saints is rooted in a love of God that is ready to trample on self. In a word, this latter relies on the Lord, whereas the other boasts that it can get along by itself. (CG 14.28)

Augustine's political philosophy is in sharp opposition to that of the Greeks, who supposed that active participation in the state was a source of fulfillment. For Augustine, the state is a necessary evil, a result of the fall. It was instituted to reign in sinful human nature, which naturally tends toward lawlessness (CG 22.22). Contrary to the vain attempts of all secular utopias, the only truly good society is the community of faithful believers that God has founded and that will reign throughout all eternity. In the meantime, God's people live out their earthly existence in the ambiguity of being part of two kingdoms. Since we live in a particular state, we owe allegiance to it insofar as it does not prevent the worship of the true God. Civil society has the virtue that it provides peace, even if a temporal and imperfect peace. Hence, the citizens of the heavenly kingdom can use the benefits of society. However, we must always realize that in this present life we are mere travelers in a foreign land, for our true home is in heaven, and only there can we find true peace (CG 19.17). Because the earthly state inevitably reflects the corruption of human nature, we must direct our lives according to the laws of the higher kingdom and seek to influence the civil society with the principles of God's kingdom. Augustine makes it clear that the Church is superior to the state because only the Church is the source of the true principles of human conduct. This view on Church–state relations was very influential in the Middle Ages. In the latter part of this age, it caused a great deal of tension as the Church and political kingdoms wrestled for dominance.

THE MEANING OF HISTORY

Augustine's view of history can be summed up in the following passage:

> It is therefore this God, the author and giver of felicity, who, being the one true God, gives earthly dominion both to good men and to evil. And he does this not at random or, as one may say, fortuitously, because he is God, not Fortune. Rather he gives in accordance with the order of events in history, an order completely hidden from us, but perfectly known to God himself. Yet God is not bound in subjection to this order of events; he is himself in control, as the master of events, and arranges the order of things as a governor. (CG-B 4.33)

Several important points lie latent within this passage. First, Augustine is uncompromising when he ascribes to God total, providential control over history. For example, he claims God established Rome:

> It was God's good pleasure, by means of this city, to subdue the whole world, to bring it into a single society of a republic under law, and to bestow upon it a widespread and enduring peace. (CG 18.22)

But this is true not only for Rome, but for all political kingdoms: "We must ascribe to the true God alone the power to grant kingdoms and empires" (CG 5.21). Augustine lists by name good kingdoms as well as evil kingdoms, just and righteous rulers along with cruel tyrants, and says they all receive their power from God (CG 5.21). He controls even the progress and outcome of wars:

The same may be said of the duration of wars. It rests with the decision of God in his just judgment and mercy either to afflict or console mankind, so that some wars come to an end more speedily, others more slowly. (CG 5.22)

Second, Augustine gives a moral interpretation of history. History is not to be understood in terms of economics or politics. Instead, these are simply the end result of the moral forces at work. For example, the Israelites prospered when they worshiped the one true God, but they suffered when they worshiped idols. When Rome prospered, it did so either because it was led by Christian emperors or by rulers who at least tried to follow justice and virtue. Rome eventually declined when its people and rulers turned to immorality. However, Augustine does not think any simple formula can make history's pattern completely transparent. It is an "order completely hidden from us." We must not think that God is not in control whenever the wicked prosper and the good suffer. Even here there is a purpose to it all, for just as fire purifies gold but consumes chaff, so the suffering of good persons serves the end of testing and purifying them, and keeps the faithful from being too attached to their physical well-being and material gain. Although the distribution of rewards and suffering may seem unjust, "in general, bad men come to a bad end, and good men enjoy eventual success" (CG 20.2).

THE PROBLEM OF PROVIDENCE AND FREE WILL IN HISTORY

Once again we face a tension that is persistent throughout Augustine's writings, this time projected from the individual person's level onto the face of history itself. If God is all powerful, is any room left for human decisions? We have been told God orchestrates the events of history to achieve his purposes for individuals and nations. Wars, brutalities, tyrants, and natural calamities, as well as economic and political prosperity and the beauty and bounty of nature, have all been provided by God to punish humanity or to bless it as he sees fit (CG 22.22,24). Once again, Augustine insists both that God is in control and that humans

are responsible. For example, he says that in ancient times God stirred up the enemies of his people to devastate them when they deserved chastisement. This raises the question: Did the invading armies do this on their own, or did God cause them to do it? Augustine's answer is "Both statements to be sure are true, because they both came by their own will, and yet the Lord stirred up their spirit" (GFW 42). However, in the final analysis it seems God is in control. "For the Almighty sets in motion even in the innermost hearts of men the movement of their will" (GFW 42).

THE IMPLICATIONS OF AUGUSTINE'S THEORY OF HISTORY

Some readers of Augustine find his view very encouraging, and others find it troubling. On the one hand, his view leads to optimism because it presents a teleological (purposeful) view of history. When faced with injustice and tremendous social upheavals, many people in Augustine's day and in our own time find it comforting to believe that history is not a collection of random events, but is an ordered series of events fulfilling a purpose.

On the other hand, along with these comforts comes the unsettling conclusion that the outcome of every human decision is already decided. Apparently, we don't make much of a difference at all, if we are merely playing a role in a play that is already written. Furthermore, if we accept Augustine's account of divine providence (things are the way they were meant to be), then we must be very cautious in trying to change the course of events. This leads to a very conservative outlook that encourages acceptance of the status quo. Accordingly, preserving peace and social order, even if it is an evil social order, are priorities for Augustine. For example, he says slavery is not part of the natural order but is the result of sin (CG 19.15). But he apparently thinks it is less serious than sexual sins: "It is better to be the slave of a man than the slave of passion." By living a life of virtue and obedience, the slave is strengthened in character, while the master is harmed by his ruthlessness. Hence, there is little room in Augustine's political theory for the American Revolution or any of the confrontational methods for achieving social change and civil rights that have brought justice to so many societies throughout history.

Evaluation and Significance

WAS AUGUSTINE A PHILOSOPHER?

Anyone who attempts to analyze Augustine's philosophical views must deal with the question of whether he can properly be said to be a philosopher at all. Many would say "No!" for he makes use of biblical authority, and too many of his discussions are replete with theological assumptions. Augustine, however, would probably agree with Simmias in Plato's dialogue *Phaedo*. In this story, Socrates and his friends are speculating about the possibility of life after death. In despair, Simmias says it is almost impossible to achieve certainty in this life about these questions. Perhaps the best we can do, he says, is "to select the best and most dependable theory which human intelligence can supply, and use it as a raft to ride the seas of life— that is, *assuming that we cannot make our journey with greater confidence and security by the surer means of divine revelation*" (emphasis added).[5] Augustine, of course, believes we do have this more sure means of arriving at our destination and need not endure the risks and uncertainties of the tenuous raft of human reason.

Despite his use of supernatural revelation, however, a case could be made that in many passages Augustine is indeed writing as a philosopher. He addressed philosophical themes such as the nature of the self, knowledge, and time, as well as the status of universal truths, the existence of God, and human immortality and provided philosophical arguments to underscore the biblical answers. Whether we think these arguments are good or not is not the issue. Since many of his arguments are clever modifications of Platonic arguments, if Augustine is not a philosopher then neither is Plato. Augustine, no doubt, would not have cared whether the final verdict was that he was only a theologian and not a philosopher. He was simply concerned to pursue the truth and to persuade others of it, using any resources available. He was writing for both a non-Christian and a Christian audience. With respect to the first audience, he realized that intellectual arguments alone would not convert the atheist any more than they had converted him. Nevertheless, the philosophical reasonings of the Neoplatonists did remove some obstacles from the threshold of faith for Augustine and started him on his journey toward God. This is what he hoped his works could do for others. For the Christian audience, he hoped to work out a Christian worldview that would show the implications and relevance of the biblical faith for all the traditional issues of philosophical and cultural concern.

AUGUSTINE'S INFLUENCE

Whether or not you agree with his conclusions, the importance of Augustine's thought is hard to overestimate. Christian thinkers preceding him tried to integrate Christian revelation and Greek philosophy, but Augustine is a pioneer in terms of the comprehensive scope of his topics. Consequently, he has served as a model of Christian scholarship throughout the Middle Ages and up to our own day. Augustine not only influenced the Roman Catholic tradition, however, for he has had a considerable impact on traditional Protestant theology as well. The Protestant Reformers thought they were doing nothing more than returning to the purity of Augustine's theology. John Calvin, the sixteenth-century Reformer, said that he could write the whole of his theology out of Augustine.

In his *City of God*, Augustine raised written history from a mere chronicle of events to the telling of a story, that seeks to reveal the meaning behind the events. Even today, some newspaper editorials and political speeches attribute the rise and fall of nations and leaders to their moral qualities. These examples show how much Augustine has influenced our ways of thinking about world events. Finally, he gave birth to many of the themes of modern philosophy and was, thereby, twelve centuries ahead of his time. His use of an introspective examination of the self as a philosophical starting point is a technique that we will not see again until the Renaissance.

Questions for Understanding

1. Why does Augustine place so much importance on the will?

2. What were Augustine's arguments against skepticism?

3. In what ways did Augustine agree and disagree with Plato?

4. Why does Augustine believe that reason can never be religiously neutral?

5. In what ways does Augustine bring in philosophical considerations in his account of creation?

6. How does Augustine view the relationship between God's foreknowledge and human freedom?

7. What is the problem of evil? In what ways does Augustine attempt to solve it?

8. According to Augustine, what is the nature of human history?

9. What are the two cities? What role do they play in Augustine's account of history?

Questions for Reflection

1. Socrates believed that people do what is wrong out of ignorance of what is really good. What would Augustine say?

2. Think about a time in your life when you made an ethical decision. Would you agree with Augustine that what we love is what determines our will and our intellect? Are there ever times when your intellect determines your will?

3. Do you agree with Augustine that if there were a God who foreknows and controls all events, that this could be consistent with your ability to make free choices? Why?

4. What do you think of Augustine's view that history is not random, but follows a pattern? Do you agree with his emphasis on history as a moral struggle between good and evil?

5. If Augustine had written a book on your country's history, what sorts of facts, events, and patterns would he emphasize?

6. Is Augustine's view of history an optimistic or pessimistic one?

Notes

1. References to the works of Augustine are abbreviated as follows:

AA   *Against the Academicians*, trans. Sister Mary Patricia Garvey (Milwaukee: Marquette University Press, 1957).

C   *Confessions*, trans. Henry Chadwick (Oxford, England: Oxford University Press, 1991).

CD   *On Christian Doctrine*, trans. J. F. Shaw in *A Select Library of the Nicene and Post-Nicene Fathers of the Christian Church*, vol. 2, ed. Philip Schaff (Buffalo, NY: The Christian Literature Company, 1887).

CG   *The City of God*, trans. Gerald G. Walsh, Demetrius B. Zema, Grace Monahan, and Daniel J. Honan (New York: Doubleday Image, 1958).

CG-B   *The City of God*, trans. Henry Bettenson (Harmondsworth, Middlesex, England: Penguin Books, 1972).

E   *Enchiridion*, trans. J. F. Shaw in *A Select Library of the Nicene and Post-Nicene Fathers of the Christian Church*, vol. 3, ed. Philip Schaff (Buffalo, NY: The Christian Literature Company, 1887).

CF   *Concerning Faith of Things Not Seen*, trans. C. L. Cornish, in *A Select Library of the Nicene and Post-Nicene Fathers of the Christian Church*, vol. 3, ed. Philip Schaff (Buffalo, NY: The Christian Literature Company, 1887).

FCW   *On Free Choice of the Will*, trans. Anna S. Benjamin and L. H. Hackstaff (New York: Macmillan, Library of Liberal Arts, 1964).

GFW   *On Grace and Free Will*, trans. Peter Holmes, Robert E. Wallis, and Benjamin B. Warfield in *A Select Library of the Nicene and Post-Nicene Fathers of the Christian Church*, vol. 5, ed. Philip Schaff (New York: The Christian Literature Company, 1887).

HT   *On the Holy Trinity*, trans. Arthur W. Haddan and W. G. T. Shedd in *A Select Library of the Nicene and Post-Nicene Fathers of the Christian Church*, vol. 3, ed. Philip Schaff (Buffalo, NY: The Christian Literature Company, 1887).

PS   *On the Predestination of the Saints*, trans. Peter Holmes, Robert E. Wallis, and Benjamin B. Warfield in *A Select Library of the Nicene and Post-Nicene Fathers of the Christian Church*, vol.

5, ed. Philip Schaff (New York: The Christian Literature Company, 1887).

SL   *Soliloquies*, trans. C. C. Starbuck in *A Select Library of the Nicene and Post-Nicene Fathers of the Christian Church*, vol. 7, ed. Philip Schaff (New York: The Christian Literature Company, 1888).

SR   *Sermons on Selected Lessons of the New Testament*, trans. R. G. MacMullen in *A Select Library of the Nicene and Post-Nicene Fathers of the Christian Church*, vol. 6, ed. Philip Schaff (New York: Scribner's, 1903).

TR   *Of True Religion*, trans. J. H. S. Burleigh (Chicago: Regnery, 1968).

2. Quoted in Armand A. Maurer, *Medieval Philosophy* (New York: Random House, 1962), 8.

3. Ecclesiasticus 18.1. This book is found in the deutero-canonical section of the Catholic Bible. The problem only occurs in the particular translation that Augustine used.

4. Wolfgang Amadeus Mozart, "A Letter" in *The Creative Process*, ed. Brewster Ghiselin (New York: New American Library, Mentor, 1963), 45.

5. Plato, *Phaedo* 85d, trans. Hugh Tredennick in *The Collected Dialogues of Plato*, ed. Edith Hamilton and Huntington Cairns (New York: Random House, Pantheon, 1961).

9

Early Medieval Philosophy

From the Roman World to the Middle Ages

Soon after Augustine's death, the philosophical stream became muddy, and many obstacles arose to dissipate its energy and confuse its direction. The rise of Christianity had brought with it a new conception of the world and a distinct philosophical agenda that forged new channels for the waters of ancient philosophy. But in the early centuries following Augustine these waters stagnated and only a few trickles of fresh philosophical thought appeared. Eventually, however, a number of intellectual, political, and cultural forces came together to form the great tributary of the Middle Ages, and the philosophical stream broke through again with new vigor. The term "Middle Ages" refers to the one thousand-year period in western Europe that falls between the classical period and the modern age. It is also known as the *medieval* period from the Latin words *medium* (middle) and *aevum* (age). This period runs roughly from the fall of Rome in the fifth century to the dramatic changes in politics, religion, philosophy, and the arts in the 1500s. Philosophically,

it can be designated as running from the time of Augustine to the Renaissance. The term "Middle Ages" was originally derogatory. It was coined by the Renaissance thinkers who saw this period as an unfortunate interval of intellectual darkness that interrupted an otherwise continuous stream of progress from the classical period to their own time. This picture eventually changed as later historians came to recognize the importance of the medieval thinkers' accomplishments.

A Survey of the Early Middle Ages

To tell the story of philosophy after Augustine, we must begin with the fall of the Roman Empire. Its collapse resulted from both internal and external problems. Internally, it could not manage its vast size and extent. The empire's ponderous bureaucracy weighed it down and required the distribution of more and more power to the local provinces. As part of the decentralization program, the empire was divided into two regions. The western empire was originally ruled from Rome, but in the early fifth century the center of power was shifted to the better-fortified Ravenna.

The eastern empire was run from Constantinople. The division started out as an administrative convenience, but became permanent, and the empire never achieved unity again.

In the west, external problems accelerated the collapse of the Roman Empire. For many centuries, Germanic tribes from northern Europe had occupied the boundaries of the Roman territories. To maintain its overextended empire the Romans resorted to recruiting non-Romans (whom they called the "barbarians") into its army. Eventually whole alien tribes began to settle within the frontiers and began to dominate the territories. In the late fourth and fifth centuries, the Germanic tribes from the north (the Vandals, Visigoths, and Ostrogoths) moved into the heart of the empire. In 410 the Goths sacked Rome, and in 455 the small but aggressive tribe known as the Vandals raided the city. Their reputation made a mark on our language, for we still refer to looters and destroyers as "vandals." Finally, in 476, the Roman Empire fell, and by the end of the fifth century the western empire was a fragmented collection of tribal kingdoms. The Vandals held North Africa, and the Goths occupied Italy and Spain. Only two of the tribes succeeded in building permanent states. The first was the Franks, who took over Gaul and the Rhineland and gave modern France its name. The second long-lived state was produced by the Angles and the Saxons, who sailed across the North Sea to conquer Britain. Later, in the tenth century, their separate states merged into the single kingdom known as England ("Angle-land"). During the six hundred years from A.D. 400 to 1000 the story of western Europe was dominated by wars and invasions. Violence and anarchy do not provide fertile grounds in which philosophy may flourish. Hence, the political instability of this time prevented any coherent culture from taking root.

THE CHURCH

In the midst of all this change and turmoil, the one institution that managed to survive was the Catholic Church. While the secular empire crumbled around it, the Church retained its cohesion and preserved its character as a central organization and universal institution. Facilitating this was the fact that by the fifth century, the Western Church took on the organizational structure of a monarchy by declaring the bishop of Rome to be the "Father of the Church" or the "Pope" (from the Latin word *papa*). In the face of the cultural vacuum left by the fallen empire, the Church gained strength as the only institution strong enough to endure the changes. Thus, on its shoulders fell the responsibility of preserving the past and shaping the future. It took over many functions that the crumbling civil government could not handle. The Church collected taxes, looked after the food supply, repaired the city walls, maintained courts of criminal law, and used its buildings for hospitals and inns. Most importantly, the Church became the center of education, even though limited to the clergy and the monks.

PERIODS OF DARKNESS AND LIGHT

Despite the remnants of cultural unity preserved by the Church, the early Middle Ages was a time when the stream of culture and philosophy was at its lowest ebb. The period running from the fall of Rome and the death of Augustine to the year 1000 is commonly called the "Dark Ages." This grim picture may result from our limited historical resources, yet the educational and cultural activities of these centuries do seem limited compared with earlier ages. A brief moment of light during these centuries was produced by Charlemagne (Charles the Great), who ruled from A.D. 768 until his death in 814. He started out as the ruler of the Frankish kingdom but ended up uniting all western Europe. He engineered a rare period known as the Carolingian Renaissance, in which education and the arts were promoted. Charlemagne started schools within the cathedrals and monasteries, which attracted scholars from all over Europe. These schools preserved the classical Christian culture of the past, both through instruction and the copying of important texts. Throughout the dark and turbulent period following his death, these schools kept the light of knowledge lit until the eleventh and twelfth centuries, when philosophy blazed brightly again. In the later Middle Ages, most of the great universities of Europe rose from the institutions that Charlemagne had founded.

The Byzantine and Islamic Empires

The eastern division of the Roman Empire came to be known as the Byzantine Empire. Unlike its factious western counterpart, it maintained a reasonable degree of cultural and political unity throughout the Middle Ages. Among the resources it inherited were the two great centers of learning: Athens and Alexandria. When the Christians had been in the minority in the old Roman Empire, they had pleaded for tolerance from the pagans. However, when the Church gained dominance, it did not follow its own moral advice. Consequently, the pagans and the Jews often suffered persecution within Christian lands. In Alexandria, a Neoplatonic school flourished, run by an accomplished female philosopher named Hypatia. In 415 she was brutally murdered by a fanatical Christian mob, who were encouraged by the repressive policies of Cyril, the local bishop. In Athens, the successor to Plato's Academy and other pagan schools continued to prosper. However, the Emperor Justinian the Great closed these schools in 529. Despite this hostility, scholars kept alive the study of Plato, Neoplatonism, and Aristotle and kept their texts from being lost for all time. However, apart from their notable achievements in art and architecture, the Byzantines' preoccupation with theological and political disputes prevented them from making any important contributions to philosophy, science, or literature.

By the eighth century, the new religion of Islam had made its mark as a cultural and political force. The Muslims took control of the eastern, southern, and western shores of the Mediterranean, including Persia, Syria, Egypt, Africa, and Spain. Thus, the heirs of the later Roman Empire were the three great civilizations of the Mediterranean world: the European, the Byzantine, and the Islamic. Of these three, the European world was the most culturally primitive until the eleventh century. The Muslims would come to play an important role in the development of philosophy, for they inherited Aristotle's texts and

eventually passed the ancient texts and a rich philosophical tradition on to Western Christianity.

An Overview of Medieval Philosophy

Before we begin to look at the philosophy of this period, it will be useful to set out a map of the terrain. Western philosophy from the beginning of the Christian era up to the close of the Middle Ages can be divided into five periods. The early period of Christian philosophy, which we examined in the last two chapters, is known as the *Patristic period*, which began in the first century A.D. and reached its apex in the philosophical and theological system of St. Augustine.* His was the last example of Christian thought born within the context of classical civilization. However, Augustine's writings were more than an epilogue to the Patristic era—they were also the prologue to the next chapter in philosophy's story. Augustine's Platonic Christianity would prove to be a dominant influence throughout the Middle Ages until the thirteenth century, when his system had to compete with alternative systems of thought based on Aristotle. This new approach would be most fully worked out by St. Thomas Aquinas, the thirteenth-century thinker who represents the culmination of medieval philosophy.

Between St. Augustine and the end of the Middle Ages lay a period of about ten centuries, an expanse of time longer than the whole classical period. This era can be divided into four periods, each of which is covered in a separate chapter. The early part of the Middle Ages (from the fifth to the end of the tenth centuries) was troubled by cultural and political upheavals, including a lot of bloodshed, as western Europe experienced the violent labor pains attending the birth of a new civilization. This period is commonly known as the *Dark Ages*. Despite the predominance of cultural darkness, there were a few bright lights during this

*"Patristic" comes from *pater*, the Latin for "father," and refers to the writings of the early Christian thinkers, who are called the "Fathers of the Church."

time. The philosophers Boethius in the early sixth century and John Scotus Erigena in the ninth century stand out as courageous voices in a time when philosophy was neglected. Charlemagne's support of education and the arts also kept alive the philosophical flame—but only barely. Nevertheless, by the ninth century Europe fell behind the classical world by every measure of civilization. The Dark Ages finally ended around the year 1000, when there was a sudden flowering, a fresh awakening of cultural life. The rediscovery of the texts of classical writers fueled the philosophical revival. As a result, we reach the *formative period* of the Middle Ages in the eleventh and twelfth centuries, which are covered in the next chapter. Here, philosophy springs to life once again, with such figures as St. Anselm, Peter Abelard, and a number of Islamic and Jewish scholars. Chapter 11 discusses the *culmination of medieval philosophy* in the thirteenth century, when the rediscovery of Aristotle's philosophy inspired the monumental work of Thomas Aquinas. Finally, Chapter 12 covers the period of the *decline of medieval thought* in the fourteenth century, which began with John Duns Scotus and William of Ockham. The decline of the Middle Ages then sets the stage for the great movements of the Renaissance and Reformation and for the rise of modern science.

Early Medieval Philosophy

Given our knowledge of the intellectual riches of the Greek philosophical tradition, it is startling to realize how few of their works were available throughout most of the medieval period. During the Roman period, Greek books were rarely translated into Latin because scholars who were interested in them could still read the originals. However, after St. Jerome translated most of the Bible into Latin (completed about A.D. 410), knowledge of Greek seemed superfluous and interest in the language declined. Furthermore, classical studies did not survive the social and political turmoil surrounding the fall of the empire. What is worse, basic skills of reading and writing were on the decline.

Because of the scarcity of Latin translations of Greek writings, the early medieval philosophers were familiar with only a few works from the classical period. Their knowledge of Plato was limited to his *Timaeus*, a work they thought pointed to the Christian view of the cosmos. The problem was, this work was a mythological cosmology that did not communicate many of the important ideas Plato's other works contained. The knowledge of Aristotle available at this time was confined to parts of his works on logic. In addition, they had an introduction to Aristotle's *Categories* written by the Neoplatonist Porphyry, a few dialogues of Cicero, and the essays of Seneca. Lucretius's poetic exposition of Epicurean atomism was available, but was not considered important, as indicated by the fact that only a single manuscript copy of his poem survived this time. Thus, until the latter part of the twelfth century, when the classics of Greek philosophy began to find their way into Europe, the early medieval scholars were limited to fragments of the Greek heritage. Although they benefited from this heritage, they were like people trying to get guidance from a jigsaw puzzle picture, but not realizing that many of the crucial pieces were missing. In addition to the poverty of philosophical resources, the times were brutal both in terms of the political violence and the physical conditions people faced. The philosophical stream had narrowed to a trickle, and the intellectual soil did not nourish philosophical fruit. As far as we can tell, there was a dearth of philosophical thinkers between the time of Augustine in the fifth century and the middle of the eleventh century. The two notable exceptions to this were the courageous and innovative figures of Boethius and John Scotus Erigena, both of whom had the rare advantage of knowing the Greek language.

BOETHIUS

Boethius (about A.D. 480–524 or 525) is commonly referred to as "the last of the Romans and the first of the medieval scholastics." His writings were an important channel through which the philosophy of the ancient world flowed into the Middle Ages. He was raised as a Christian in the home of a politically prominent Roman family. While in Athens, where he had been sent for his education, he mastered the Greek language (a rare accomplishment by the sixth century) and was exposed to the leading Greek philosophical traditions. He made it his life's goal to translate the whole of Plato's and Aristotle's works into Latin and to write commentaries on them. In addition, he thought he could harmonize their teachings. However, he did not get as far as he had hoped. If he had finished his task, the complete works of Plato and Aristotle would have been made available in Latin, and medieval philosophy would have developed quite differently from the way it did. We do know Boethius translated Aristotle's writings on logic into Latin and wrote commentaries on them. He also translated and provided several commentaries on the *Introduction to Aristotle's Categories* written by the Neoplatonist Porphyry. Furthermore, he wrote several original treatises on logic of his own, as well as five theological works. Through his scholarship, the medieval scholars learned to reason after the fashion of Aristotelian logic. In addition to his scholarly work, he held a high political office. Although he had received numerous honors, he fell out of favor and was executed on charges of high treason.

During the year he spent in prison awaiting his execution, he wrote *The Consolation of Philosophy*. This was widely read in the Middle Ages and influenced a number of writers. The theme of this work was one he had learned from the Stoics: The contemplation of abstract philosophy brings personal peace. Written in both poetry and prose, the book is a dialogue between the author and Philosophy, who is personified as a majestic but nurturing woman. Their conversation deals with a problem that was very real to Boethius: why a just man can suffer unjustly, while the wicked prosper. The answer he finds draws deeply from the wells of Plato, Aristotle, the Stoics, Plotinus, and Augustine, among others. The gist is that happiness cannot come through external fortune. Since the wicked foolishly pursue the false goods of honor, fame, riches, and bodily pleasure, they will not

find happiness. Happiness is to be found beyond this world and is available to the virtuous alone.

In the course of the discussion, he addresses the themes of human freedom and divine providence. He strives to resolve the apparent contradiction between these two propositions: (1) human action is free, and (2) God foreknows everything we will do. Boethius provides what became a classic solution to the problem. For us, he says, there cannot be any infallible foreknowledge of free actions because they have not yet been decided. However, God's relationship to time is different from ours. He does not exist in time, but experiences our past, present, and future as simultaneous moments in his eternal present. Thus, the actions you will perform in the future are already present to him, and they are known by him as your free actions. Just as your knowledge that the sun is currently rising does not determine it to rise, so God's timeless foreknowledge of your free acts does not make them determined.

Throughout this book, Boethius's tone is religious but not explicitly Christian. It was the favorite reading of such literary figures as Dante, Boccaccio, and Chaucer. It contributed to the discussion of faith and reason by working out a natural philosophy based on unaided human reason. Although his works were neglected in the centuries immediately following his death, they guided eleventh-century thinkers when philosophical thought finally revived. The singular significance of Boethius's writings and translations was that they transmitted to the Middle Ages a great deal of the available knowledge concerning Aristotle, and they showed how philosophical categories could be applied to theology. Boethius provided the basic philosophical terms, definitions, and distinctions so important to later writers. Although he suffered in his own time, later generations of medieval scholars considered his works classics and authoritative philosophical resources.

JOHN SCOTUS ERIGENA

We have very few historical records of original philosophical work occurring in the six centuries between Boethius and St. Anselm in the eleventh century. John Scotus Erigena, who lived and died from around 810 to 877, was one of the few philosophers whose work survives. He was born in Ireland and received his education at an Irish monastery.* Ireland had the happy fate of being remote and thus distant from most of the turmoil of the sixth, seventh, and eighth centuries that swept across Europe. The Irish monasteries were centers of learning where a knowledge of Greek was still valued even as it became virtually unknown in the rest of the world. Erigena is universally recognized as having written the first great complete system of philosophy of the Middle Ages, a particularly remarkable accomplishment given the poverty of philosophical works he had available to him. A decisive factor in his originality, no doubt, as well as an important influence on his outlook was the fact that he was unique among his European contemporaries in being able to use what Greek sources were available as an intellectual resource.

Erigena served for years in the court of King Charles the Bald (Charlemagne's grandson), where he was appointed head of the Palace School in France. Erigena appeared to have not only a keen intellect but a sharp wit. After Erigena and King Charles had enjoyed several rounds of strong drink, the king attempted to make fun of the Irish fondness for drink by asking his companion whether anything separated a Scot from a sot. "Only this dinner table," was Erigena's sharp reply. Because of his respect for Erigena's scholarship, Charles commissioned him to translate into Latin the writings of some of the Greek Fathers of the Church. Included among these were a number of writings attributed to Dionysius the Areopagite, who was one of St. Paul's converts, mentioned in Acts 17:34. In these manuscripts, the author gives a decidedly Neoplatonic interpretation of Christianity. Because of their alleged authorship, these writings were accepted by medieval scholars as having almost apostolic authority and were very

well read throughout the medieval period. Much later, however, around the seventeenth century, they were discovered to be forgeries, now attributed to an unknown sixth-century Syrian Neoplatonist whom we now call "Pseudo-Dionysius." Nevertheless, their influence helped impose a Neoplatonic and mystical outlook on the philosophy and theology of the next six centuries. Furthermore, the ideas of Pseudo-Dionysius set the framework for all of Erigena's constructive philosophy.

For Erigena, the goal of philosophy was simply to provide a rational interpretation of revelation. The later medieval understanding of the differing tasks of philosophy and theology would not have occurred to him. Accordingly, he quotes Augustine to support his thesis that "true philosophy is true religion, and conversely, true religion is true philosophy."[1] True to the Christian tradition, Erigena affirms that Sacred Scripture should be followed in all things, but he recognizes it requires interpretation if we are to understand what it says. For Erigena, there are two sources for interpreting Scripture: reason and the Church Fathers. But he emphasizes the priority of reason, for he says that

> Authority indeed proceeds from true reason, reason never proceeds from authority. For all authority which true reason does not endorse is seen to be weak. True reason, however, being ratified and rendered immutable by virtue of itself, needs no additional assent from authority to strengthen it. (DN 1.69)[2]

In saying this, however, he was not brushing aside the authority of the Church Fathers in the name of sovereign, secular reason. Instead, he had faith that true authority and true reason would not conflict on the main issues since they "both spring from a common source, namely, divine wisdom" (DN 1.66).[3] If reason and authority seem to conflict, then one or the other is not genuine. Nevertheless, this methodological stance freed him to interpret both revelation and the doctrinal tradition in the directions his philosophical reason led him.

This approach is evident in his greatest work, *On the Division of Nature*, which was published about 867. The "Nature" referred to in the title embraces the whole of reality, including God and

---

*Although he was Irish, his name means "John the Scot," for during the early Middle Ages Ireland was known as Scotia. "Erigena," the latter part of his name, meant "of the people of Erin."

his creation. He says Nature has four aspects, which collectively exhaust all the logical possibilities: (1) What creates and is not created (God as the cause of things but who is himself without cause); (2) what creates and is created: the ideas in the Divine Logos, which form the blueprints and primordial causes of all created beings (Erigena's version of the Platonic Forms); (3) what is created but does not create: the created universe itself; and (4) what neither creates nor is created: this is God again, but now viewed as the final end of the creative process. Erigena believed all things would return to their source and be reunited in the being of God. There seems to be little doubt that Erigena's intentions were always to be an orthodox theologian. But he persistently tended to blur the distinction between (1) pantheism (which emphasizes the immanence of God to the point of identifying God and the world) and, in contrast, (2) biblical theism (which protects the transcendence of God and the creator creation distinction). How he saw these two elements as cohering is one of the main problems in understanding him.

Numerous recurring passages in Erigena have all the trademarks of pantheism. Given his Neoplatonic assumptions, it would have been virtually impossible for Erigena to have stuck with the orthodox doctrine that God is absolutely separate from creation. For example, the Neoplatonism he absorbed from Pseudo-Dionysius dictated that the only way one could conceive of the world as depending on God was to suppose the world *participates* in the being of God or *flows* from it. Quoting the authority of the author he thought was Dionysius, he says God "is called the One because He is all things universally; for there is nothing in existence which does not participate in the One" (DN 3.8).[4] Going even further, Erigena asserts that the One "extends Itself into everything and the extension itself *is* everything" (DN 3.9).[5] There could not be a clearer expression of the identity of God and the world. Erigena argues that there can be no accidents in God, meaning that every aspect of God's nature and all that proceeds from it are necessary. Thus, the universe is a necessary fulfillment of the divine creativity, just as the infinite number series is a rationally neces-

sary procession from its source in the number 1. Without the universe, God would only be a potential creator and thus unfulfilled and defective. If the universe does not flow necessarily from the nature of God, then creation is just an arbitrary and capricious whim on his part. The rational necessity of creation and its comparison to the unfolding of the number series looks back to the Neoplatonist Plotinus and looks forward to the great seventeenth-century metaphysician Spinoza, both of whom are sometimes interpreted as pantheists. Similarly, Erigena frequently uses the Neoplatonic metaphor that God's being is like a river that flows into everything, while the waters remain the same (DN 3.4).[6]

This view of God raises the problem of evil. If the universe is an outflowing of God's being, then why is evil in the world? With Augustine, Erigena believed that just as darkness is not a positive entity in itself but the absence of light, so evil is the absence of good. He also borrows from Augustine the explanation that our experience of evil is due to our limited view of the universe. He quotes Augustine's point that what appears to be evil is like the shadows in a painting. Seen by themselves, they are ugly, but in the context of the whole, they help create the beauty of the painting.

In his account of the fourth division or the final phase of nature's cycle, Erigena speculates that all distinctions and fragmentation will eventually be overcome, for these are the result of a lapse from the unity of God's being. Just as all things originally flow from God's being without diminishing it, so all things will eventually return to the same unity without enriching it. All the longings we feel in our earthly existence are really expressions of the desire to be unified with God again. This account reflects the Greek tendency to absorb all things into eternity. However, it diminishes the significance of time and creation, which are essential features of a Christian perspective. Even one of Erigena's most sympathetic commentators complains about this theory that

> It seems to be impossible to retain the reality of the
> temporal universe in any satisfying sense. For when
> all has been reabsorbed into the Absolute, what has

the cosmic process accomplished? What is different be-
cause anything did ever exist? What has been achieved
by the immense structure of the creation, by all the
labour and experience and suffering of humanity?[7]

A further difficulty with the notion that all things
are absorbed into the unity of God is that it raises
problems for the Christian doctrine of immortality.
Although Erigena tries very hard to preserve individual immortality, his Neoplatonism always seems
to dilute it. For example, he says that at the end of
time, "every creature will be cast into the shade,
i.e. changed into God, as the stars at the rising of
the sun" (DN 3.23).[8]

One of the most interesting issues raised by
Erigena is in a passage inspired by Pseudo-
Dionysius where Erigena argues that God is above
and beyond all categories of being and thought,
for to describe him would be to limit him
(DN 1.10-14).[9] In this passage Erigena raises the
problem of religious language, a problem philosophers of religion wrestled with from this time on
into the twentieth century. The problem is, how can
we use words and concepts drawn from our finite,
earthbound experience to describe an infinite and
transcendent being? Borrowing from Pseudo-
Dionysius, Erigena's solution is to use both affirmative theology and negative theology. When we
affirm that "God is good," we must keep in mind
that our human notion of goodness is not adequate
to God, so we must immediately add, "God is not
good" (for it would be unseemly to suppose that
God shares anything in common with finite,
human goodness). All our affirmative statements
about God are necessarily metaphorical, for human
concepts do not do him justice. However, when we
are saying what God is *not*, this negative theology
may be taken literally. Erigena's (and Pseudo-
Dionysius's) final solution is to speak of God only
by means of superlative theology. We can say that
God is Supertruth, God is Superwisdom, God is
Supergood, and so on, thus avoiding the sugges-
tion that his properties bear any similarity to their
earthly counterparts. Although we can use these
phrases, we cannot have a conceptual understanding of what Supergoodness is other than to know it
is superior to ordinary, human concepts and exam-

ples of goodness. The situation is like trying to describe a three-dimensional sphere using only the
terminology of plane geometry. We could say the
sphere is circular but it is not a circle. It contains an
infinite number of circles, yet is more than just a
two-dimensional collection of many circles. Since
such a God cannot be apprehended intellectually,
mystical experience seems the only way to approach him. Thus, even Erigena's attempt to emphasize the transcendence of God forces him to fall
back on a Neoplatonic merging with God in mystical experience. Because of the powerful way in
which he presents his vision of God, John Scotus
Erigena became an important source of inspiration
to the later tradition of Christian mysticism as well
as to some of the heretical sects in the twelfth and
thirteenth centuries.

Despite the abundance of Neoplatonic elements
in his thinking (many of which are at odds with traditional Christian theology), Erigena did not see
himself as anything but an orthodox theologian. He
tries very hard to reconcile his position with Scripture and continually quotes the Church Fathers, especially Augustine. Furthermore, he frequently
reminds us that all his language about God is necessarily metaphorical. To be fair to him, his more
pantheistic statements must be balanced with those
in which he affirms a radical distinction between
God and creation. Nevertheless, Erigena's opinion
on his own orthodoxy was not shared by the ecclesiastical authorities. Eventually his book was condemned as pantheistic heresy and all copies
ordered to be burned in 1225 by Pope Honorious
III, who described it as "swarming with worms of
heretical perversity." Earlier, another of his works
was condemned by the Council of Valence (855) as
"Irish porridge" and "the devil's invention."

Even though in his heart Erigena aimed at orthodoxy, his Neoplatonic ideas veered in directions
he did not intend. This created problems not only
for him but for the whole medieval Church. On
the one hand, the writings of Pseudo-Dionysius
were thought to be authentic and authoritative. On
the other hand, Neoplatonism and Christian orthodoxy pull in different directions on many issues. The Church saw that Erigena's conclusions
were heretical, but it was not clear how to avoid

them because Neoplatonism was the only philosophical resource available at that time for Christian thinkers. Consequently, in the next couple of centuries after John Scotus Erigena, no one attempted to take up his task of constructing a comprehensive metaphysical system. Instead, Christian philosophers focused their attention on more isolated and manageable philosophical problems. What was lacking was a different model to guide philosophical thought. Philosophers needed a system that would preserve the otherworldly, eternal, and universal elements that were important to Christian theology, while doing justice to this world, the reality of time, and the existence of particulars. Accordingly, when Aristotle's metaphysical manuscripts became available in Europe in the twelfth century, it was possible to begin a new approach to systematic philosophy. Until then, we find philosophers sticking with piecemeal analyses of technical problems.

The Return to Darkness

Despite his courageous and innovative philosophical speculations, the lone voice of John Scotus Erigena did not have much of an impact. Furthermore, the intellectual and cultural momentum created by Charlemagne slowed to a halt after his death in 814. Once again, tribal monarchies arose to fill the political vacuum and a fragmented Europe lay helpless as the invasions began again with a new vigor. The Vikings with their military savagery and enormous sea power raided Europe and wrecked havoc in Hamburg, Paris, and Bordeaux, while the Muslim Saracens invaded Italy. Furthermore, it was a degrading time for the Church, because corruption and control by local political factions dictated the character of the Church at this time. From the years 800 to 1000, the age seemed committed to political instability, corruption, invasions, and violence. While Muslim culture continued to flourish, the rest of western Europe sank to the lowest depths it had ever experienced. Physical conditions were severe as war, disease, and famine set the agenda for people's daily lives. The average person lived only thirty years and fewer than 20 percent of the people

traveled more than 10 miles from their birthplace. During the roughly 150 years from the death of Erigena to the birth of Anselm, there is no record of any significant philosophical voice. Thus began the second Dark Ages in Europe, the darkest of its kind.

Questions for Understanding

1. What are the five periods of Western philosophy in the time frame ranging from the beginning of the Christian era to the close of the Middle Ages?

2. What works of Greek philosophy were available to the early medieval philosophers? What were the effects of this limited knowledge of previous philosophies?

3. What philosophical issues concerned Boethius?

4. How did John Scotus Erigena view the relationship of faith and reason?

5. In what ways did Neoplatonic philosophy influence Erigena's metaphysics?

6. What is the problem of religious language and how did Erigena attempt to solve it?

7. Why did Erigena's contemporaries reject his philosophy?

8. What factors led to the decline of philosophy in the 150 years following the death of Erigena?

Questions for Reflection

1. What are the strengths and weaknesses of Boethius's solution to the problem of divine foreknowledge versus human freedom?

2. How did Erigena's Neoplatonism lead him to pantheism?

3. What are the strengths and weaknesses of Erigena's solution to the problem of religious language?

Notes

1. On Predestination, chap. 1, trans. Allan B. Wolter, in *Medieval Philosophy: From St. Augustine to Nicholas of Cusa*, ed. John F. Wipple and Allan B. Wolter (New York: Macmillan, Free Press, 1969), 111.

2. John Scotus Erigena, *On the Division of Nature*, trans. A. B. Wolter, in Wipple and Wolter, 113–114. All references

to Erigena's book are symbolized in the text as "DN," followed by the chapter and section numbers of the original text.

3. Wipple and Wolter, 114.

4. *Periphyseon: On the Division of Nature*, trans. Myra L. Uhlfelder (Indianapolis: Bobbs-Merrill, Library of Liberal Arts, 1976), 149.

5. Ibid., 152.

6. Ibid., 139.

7. Henry Bett, *Johannes Scotus Erigena: A Study in Medieval Philosophy* (New York: Russell & Russell, 1964), 143.

8. Quoted in Frederick Copleston, *A History of Philosophy* vol. 2, pt. 1 (Garden City, NY: Doubleday, Image Books, 1962), 148.

9. Wipple and Wolter, 122–131.

10

Philosophy and Theology in the Eleventh and Twelfth Centuries

The Flowering of the Middle Ages

By the year 1000 the near anarchy and succession of barbarian invasions that had characterized the early Middle Ages had all but passed. During the following centuries, the political, social, and economic institutions of western Europe achieved a stability and coherence that lasted for some five hundred years. The institutions, art, architecture, music, literature, and customs that developed during these centuries form the collection of images most people associate with the Middle Ages. During the period from about 1000 to the late 1200s, medieval civilization reached its highest point of achievement. For this reason, this era is commonly called "the high Middle Ages."

The fresh spirit of this age is symbolized by the rise of the Gothic cathedral. Earlier methods of church architecture had produced squat, massive, earthbound structures that suggested stone fortresses designed to protect the sacred interior from the secular world outside. In contrast, new engineering techniques enabled the roofs to soar to unheard-of heights and replaced large areas of the stone walls with radiant sheets of stained glass. The slender, skeletal structure of the rib vaulting replaced interior columns and heavy walls. This produced the illusion that the building was almost weightless and supported by the heavens themselves, giving the cathedrals a magical, mystical quality. The central device of the pointed arch not only made the vertical lines more graceful, but almost resembled a pair of hands touching in prayer.

The Gothic cathedral can serve as a symbol of the philosophical endeavors of this time. The fundamental structure of each building was based on the unyielding and universal laws of geometry and physics. But within these boundaries there was a freedom to explore a multitude of designs. The sacred worship within the buildings was illuminated by the light flowing in from the outside as it filtered through the brilliant colors and intricate designs produced by the stained-glass artisan. Similarly, medieval thought was carried on within the firm structure of Christian revelation, while the light of human reason flowed into Christian thought filtered through the patterns of Platonic and Aristotelian philosophy.

The magnificent, soaring designs of the Gothic cathedrals were achieved by orchestrating and

The interior of Chartres Cathedral, completed in 1220. The architects of medieval cathedrals used stone and stained glass to create a sense of transcendence, lifting the eyes and the heart toward the realm of the spirit. Similarly, medieval philosophers created magnificent conceptual structures out of the building blocks of ideas to point the intellect to God.

resolving opposing tensions within the arches. The earthly materials of stone and the sensuous appeal of beauty pointed beyond themselves and led the eyes and hearts of the people toward heaven. Likewise, the philosophies of the time used the tools of logic to resolve the tensions between faith and reason. This was accomplished by fitting them into their proper places within awe-inspiring conceptual structures that pointed the intellect to God.

A major cause of the burst of new intellectual energy in the high Middle Ages was the rise of universities. During the chaotic centuries following the fall of Rome, there had been a real danger that learning and scholarship would vanish from Europe. It was the monasteries that preserved intellectual culture in the West. They were repositories of precious manuscripts and provided education

to the clergy—the only people thought to need it. In the 800s Charlemagne revived interest in scholarship and the arts. As a result, cathedral schools began to develop in the towns to meet the growing interest in education. The medieval universities grew from these schools as well as from the Italian municipal schools. In the thirteenth century, universities flourished at Paris, Bologna, Naples, Montpellier, Oxford, and Cambridge, to name just a few. By the year 1500 the number of universities exceeded eighty, and many of them still exist today. We still retain many academic traditions that originated with the medieval universities, such as wearing academic robes, granting various academic degrees, and defending written theses.

The importance of the university movement for medieval philosophy is that the universities brought together groups of scholars who preserved the great ideas of the past and advanced knowledge by analyzing the arguments of important texts and debating the significant intellectual issues of the day. As a part of their education, the students were expected to take positions on different issues and defend them against the questioning of their peers and professor. The faculty were under similar pressures, for a teacher who shirked answering a difficult question could be fined or lose his students to a rival. Tradition and orthodoxy still reigned supreme, but this emphasis on questioning, controversy, argument, and debate helped produce a sense of intellectual rigor and a greater openness to new alternatives than existed previously.

Although famine, disease, violence, and ignorance remained inescapable realities in medieval life, these centuries did not lack emotional and intellectual compensations. Life had coherence, purpose, and order. The medieval people had one true faith and one Church with one supreme head, the pope. There was one political system (feudalism) and a dominant economic system (manorial agriculture). There was an established social structure made up of commoners, clergy, and nobility, each fulfilling his or her proper functions. With the earth at the center of the universe and covered by the canopy of the heavens, people had a sense of belonging to a comfortable scheme of things. Although philosophers felt free to explore uncharted intellectual waters, they were not like sailors set adrift on a starless night with no sense of direction, for they had the beacon lights of revelation and tradition to guide their intellectual journeys. Every event in life was divinely ordained, and every person, no matter how humble in social status or intellect, could aspire to a heavenly reward. Thus, the Church offered a unified and comprehensive vision of the cosmos and each person's place within it.

The Rise of Scholasticism

THE NATURE OF SCHOLASTICISM

Scholasticism is the name given to the significant intellectual movement that arose in Europe at this time. Its proponents were called *Schoolmen* or *Scholastics*. Originally the term *Scholastic* applied to anyone who learned or taught in the schools Charlemagne first established back in the eighth century. Eventually *Scholasticism* came to refer to the intellectual project of integrating faith and reason. Although a few theologians were suspicious of philosophical reason, the Scholastics' optimistic rationalism dominated the thought of the Middle Ages.

The unifying purpose of all the Scholastics was to harmonize Church doctrines and the fruits of philosophical speculation. Their philosophies were guided by their faith and their faith was interpreted in terms of their philosophies. To the Scholastics, as Peter Damian (1007–1072) expressed it, theology was the "Queen of the Sciences" and philosophy was her handmaiden. In Scholastic thought, faith guided reason, set its agendas, and gave it the main outlines and landmark truths around which philosophers could build their systems. In turn, Greek philosophy equipped them with tools for elucidating, explaining, and providing rational support for the truths of Scripture. In the early centuries of Christianity, the Patristics had their hands full trying to formulate and systematize the articles of faith. By the time Scholasticism arose, however, there was a fixed body of established doctrine and an organized Church hierarchy to protect the established doctrines. Thus, the teachings of the Church provided the unquestioned framework within which all philosophy had to find its place. Nevertheless, within these bounds the scholar's mind was free to roam and to work out alternative explanations and implications of the revealed truth. The fact that competing philosophical positions arose within the Scholastic movement showed that theology did not dictate all the answers to philosophers.

The method of Scholasticism was the dialectic, a form of argument adapted from Aristotle's works. It was a form of disputation and discussion in which first a problem was framed in the form of a question, such as "Is the existence of God self-evident?" Next, the arguments for and against the different answers were set out. Finally, some resolution was arrived at that either found a balance between the competing positions or defended the truth of one position while refuting the others.

The Scholastics had complete confidence in the power of reason to reach truth, but always balanced this with a reliance on the accepted authorities. These authorities were the Sacred Scriptures, the Church Fathers (especially Augustine), and Boethius's logical commentaries. In later centuries the discovery of Aristotle's complete works and those of his Arab commentators provided additional resources for thought. The way in which the medieval thinkers' philosophizing revolved around authoritative texts is dramatically illustrated by Peter Abelard's treatment of the problem of universals. He discusses the issue in his *Glosses on Porphyry*, which is actually his commentary on Boethius's commentary on Porphyry's commentary on Aristotle's writings on logic!

Although the Scholastics were united in seeking to work out the philosophical implications of their faith, the details of working out this vision provoked controversies that raged throughout the monasteries and universities. Three issues particularly concerned them: (1) the problem of universals, (2) the relation between faith and reason, and (3) the relation of the will to the intellect.

THE CONTROVERSY OVER UNIVERSALS

A leading philosophical controversy during the Middle Ages was the problem of universals. This problem, of course, arose within Greek philosophy with the contrasting positions of Plato and Aristotle, among others. However, the medieval thinkers saw the issue as loaded with theological implications. A universal is something that can be common to many particular things. As such, universals are important elements within our speech and thought about the world. However, a problem arises when we try to get clear about the metaphysical status of universals, for the question may be asked, What relationship do universals have to reality? For the medievals, the problem was provoked by Boethius's translation of Porphyry's *Introduction to Aristotle's Categories*. Porphyry asks three questions about universals:

1. Whether universals
   a. exist in reality independently
      or
   b. exist in the understanding alone

2. If they exist in reality, whether they are
   a. immaterial
      or
   b. material

3. Whether they
   a. are separate from sensible objects
      or
   b. are not separate from sensible objects

Concerning his own position on these questions, Porphyry replied, "I shall refuse to say. . . . Questions of this sort are most exalted business and require very great diligence of inquiry."[1] However, his warning about the difficulty of the problem did not deter the medieval scholars at all, for they believed a number of important theological issues hung on the answer.

To understand the issue facing the medieval thinkers, consider the statement "Socrates is a human." It is clear enough to what I am referring when I use the name "Socrates," but to what am I referring when I use the universal term "human"? I could be referring to the Form or Essence of Humanity (as Plato thought), or I could be merely making a sound that refers to a collection of individuals. Then again, I could be referring to an idea or concept in my mind that is applicable to Socrates. In the first case the universal would have a reality apart from the minds that think it, in the second case it would have merely verbal existence as a sound in our language, and for the third theory it would exist as a mental construction in the mind.

Extreme realism was the position taken by many of the early medieval thinkers. The term "realism" follows from the fact that they believed universals are real things that exist in the world. Hence, from the alternatives listed by Porphyry, they affirmed that (1a) universals exist in reality, and (2a) they are immaterial. The most extensive version went on to affirm the Platonic thesis (3a) that universals are separate from the particular individuals that manifest them. John Scotus Erigena, for example, accepted the Neoplatonic story that the forms exist as intermediaries between God and the physical world. Likewise, St. Anselm in the eleventh century adhered fairly closely to the Platonic view, although he was much more theologically orthodox than Erigena. Most, like William of Champeaux (1070–1121), did not think it necessary to postulate that universals exist independently of individual things. Nevertheless, he believed that the same universal existed within each individual of a species. For example, Bob, Desmond, Sabrina, and Kathy all contain the full essence of humanity. The differences between individuals (hair color, height, and so on) are minor modifications of their essential humanity.

A number of factors led the realists to their position. First, there was an epistemological motivation. Since the eleventh-century thinkers based all their reasoning on Aristotle's logic, they assumed that reasoning proceeded by setting out the logical relationships between universals. Accordingly, if universals do not name real things, then we are reasoning about fictions and we have no knowledge. They were convinced that there must be a one-to-one correspondence between reason and reality. However, theological issues were also at stake. Realism helped make the doctrine of original sin intelligible.* According to the theologian Odo of Tournai (died 1113), who was an extreme realist, humanity consists of a singular nature or universal essence in which we all participate. When the first man and woman sinned, this essence became infected. Since we all participate in this same essence, the infection is passed on to all generations. A further consideration was that the doctrine of the Trinity seemed to require realism. How can the Father, Son, and Holy Spirit be three persons, but one God? The answer is that the divine essence is a single, universal substance, manifested in three particular persons.

Despite these theological considerations, there was a problem with realism. It claimed that indi-

vidual persons participate in the universal of Humanity, but this means that Humanity is included in the universal of Mammal, which is a part of the universal of Animal. Finally (to follow out the logic of this position), everything is subsumed within the reality of the most comprehensive universal, which would be Being itself, the one substance common to all things. But if Being is identical to God, then all things are a part of God and the distinction between God and the world collapses. This sort of pantheism was explicit in John Scotus Erigena. However, most thinkers at this time seemed unaware of this radical implication of their position. Unfortunately, these early thinkers did not have any of Plato's writings except for the *Timaeus*, and until the thirteenth century they had none of Aristotle's criticisms of Platonism. Hence, they were oblivious to many pitfalls of their position that had been identified some fourteen centuries before this current debate.

Nominalism was the other extreme position adopted on this controversy. According to nominalism (from *nomina*, the Latin for "names"), universals are merely names and only individuals are real. To the nominalist, no such thing as "redness" exists apart from particular things such as a red apple, a red sunset, or a red rose. The most extreme version of this view was probably articulated by Roscelin (about 1050–1120), a teacher of logic in France. He was condemned by the Church as a heretic, so we don't know much about him or his views. (The writings of heretics are rarely allowed to survive to tell their own story to history.) Apparently he taught that nothing exists outside of the mind except particulars and that universals do not refer to any independent realities, but are merely names or "vocal winds" (*flatus vocis*) we use to designate groups of particular things. Roscelin would, no doubt, note the absurdity of the statement "I love humanity, it's just people I can't stand." To the nominalist, there is no such thing as "humanity." It is just a shorthand verbal sign we use to stand for Malcolm, Karen, Andrea, George, . . . and the rest of the list of existing human beings. A philosophical problem with this theory was that it seemed to make universals arbitrary and subjective. On what grounds do we give the name "human" to a

---

*This doctrine states that when the first human beings (Adam and Eve) disobeyed God, sin and its consequences became an intrinsic part of the human condition.

collection of particulars if nothing makes these individuals members of the same category except for our assigning them the same label? In addition to this commonsense objection that things in the world seem divided into natural kinds, most medieval thinkers believed that their theology implied an objective order to reality, an order the nominalists seemed to deny. Furthermore, nominalism seemed to undermine the notion of original sin. If each person is unique and separate from Adam, how could his moral transgressions affect us? As for the Trinity, Roscelin consistently concluded that if there is no common essence of divinity, then the Father, Son, and Holy Spirit must be three Gods. The term "Trinity" is merely a sound referring to this collection of individuals. His tri-theism resulted in his being condemned by the Council of Soissons in 1092. Faced with possible excommunication, Roscelin abandoned his position.

Conceptualism was a position that sought a compromise between the first two extremes. This position was introduced by Peter Abelard (1079–1142). Abelard studied under Roscelin as well as William of Champeaux and found weaknesses in both of their extreme positions. Abelard argued that realism implies that universals can have mutually inconsistent qualities. For example, since the universal *animal* is present both in Socrates and a donkey, the substance *animal* is at the same time both rational and irrational. Furthermore, how can two individual men, such as Socrates standing in one place and Plato standing in another place, really be one and the same substance of humanity, as extreme realism seemed to require? Abelard also exposed the pantheism implicit within extreme realism. In response to these criticisms from his student, William modified his position, but not enough to satisfy Abelard. Abelard also attacked nominalism. Accepting Aristotle's definition that a universal is what can be predicated of many things, he argued that universals cannot be simply words, since words are physical sounds and one physical thing cannot be predicated of another thing.

To avoid these problems, Abelard explained that a universal word in itself is just a sound, but it gets its power from the fact that it points to a universal concept. The concept is the word's logical content, significance, or meaning. He says that by means of universal ideas the mind "conceives a common and confused image of many things. . . . When I hear *man* a certain figure arises in my mind which is so related to individual men that it is common to all and proper to none."[2] By suggesting that universals are indistinct and confused images, he makes them similar to the abstract visual image you get when you squint your eyes so that all you can tell is that there is a man before you, but you cannot identify him because of a lack of distinguishing features.

If we take Abelard to be saying that universals are nothing more than general concepts in the mind, then they are simply mental constructions and have no place in reality. Some commentators therefore assign the label of *moderate nominalism* to his position. However, he goes on to say that a universal conception is obtained by abstracting features that are common among several individuals. Hence, universals refer to objective features of things, but are not independent realities apart from things. For example, Socrates and Plato are the same insofar as they are both human, and this identity is found, not in some singular reality outside the mind (as the extreme realists thought), nor in the same sound we apply to each (as the nominalists thought), but in the fact that the same mental concept can be applied to each based on the similar properties they have.

Universals can be *considered separately* from individuals, but they are not genuinely *separate*. Thus Socrates' humanity is one thing and Plato's humanity is another thing, but their objective likeness is the basis of the universal concept of "human." Abelard's position undermined the appeal of extreme realism by showing that someone could deny there is one, identical essence in all members of a species, without denying objectivity to universals. The aspect of his thought that emphasizes the abstraction of objective similarities points in the direction of a moderate realism, a position more fully developed by later thinkers.

Moderate realism became the most favored resolution of the problem of universals for the late medievals.* Abelard was groping his way toward it, but the position became more clearly articulated by thinkers such as Aquinas once Aristotle's complete works were reintroduced to Western thought. Basically, this position claimed that universal ideas are formed by the mind, but are based on the objective features of extramental reality. It was the paradigm of the Scholastic project of finding a synthesis of opposing positions. With the extreme realists, the moderate realists taught that universals are before things (*ante rem*) as patterns in God's mind. With Aristotle, they said that universals exist in things (*in rem*) as properties that make individual things alike. With Aristotle and the conceptualists, they taught that universals are after things (*post rem*) as concepts within the mind formed by abstracting from individual similarities. Finally, with the nominalists they shared the disposition of seeing the individual as the ultimate unit of reality.

THE CONTROVERSY OVER FAITH AND REASON

The second problem dividing the medieval thinkers was one that had haunted the Church Fathers: How do we understand the relationship between the two sources of knowledge—faith and reason? At least five approaches to the question emerged during the Middle Ages. First, some people had complete confidence in reason and let their intellect lead their faith. Among the early thinkers who took this approach were John Scotus Erigena, Roscelin, and Abelard. The last two got into trouble because of their position, and all had their theological works condemned. Second, others tried to swing the pendulum away from reason by giving priority to faith. With the reforms of monastic life introduced around the year 1000, a resurgence of piety led some to see reason as a threat. Peter Damian (1007–1072) was one of the strongest

*The discussion of universals is complicated by the fact that not all scholars draw the boundaries between positions in the same way, nor do they use the terminology in the same way. Further confusion is caused by the fact that it is sometimes not clear what a particular philosopher's position is. This explains why different commentators call Abelard a *moderate nominalist*, a *conceptualist*, or a *moderate realist*.

voices in this movement. He warned of the "blind foolhardiness of these pseudointellectuals who investigate nonproblems" and who presume to diminish the power of God with their trust in puny logic and "arguments based on the meaning of words."[3] Similarly, for St. Bernard of Clairvaux (1091–1153), a mystic and moral reformer, philosophy was useless and a danger to the unwary. Consequently, he was the prosecutor at Abelard's heresy trial. Contrary to attempts to make the faith conform to reason, Bernard said, "I believe though I do not comprehend, and I hold by faith what I cannot grasp with the mind."[4] Third, some, such as St. Anselm, were more moderate and sought for a compromise. Anselm believed that reason could not be autonomous, for faith must lead and reason must follow. At the same time, his confidence in reason went further than that of any other Christian philosopher, for he actually thought he could deductively prove all the major Christian doctrines that he first believed on faith. Although he had a great deal of confidence in reason, he made clear that it must always operate within the bounds of orthodoxy:

> No Christian ought in any way to dispute the truth of what the Catholic Church believes in its heart and confesses with its mouth. But always holding the same faith unquestioningly, loving it and living by it, he ought . . . so far as he is able to seek the reasons for it.[5]

Fourth, St. Thomas Aquinas in the thirteenth century sought a synthesis of faith and reason. He very firmly distinguished between the spheres of theology and philosophy. Thomas believed that our limited minds could not perceive the rationality of some theological doctrines. Thus, many of the doctrines Anselm tried to prove Thomas considered mysteries that can only be known through revelation and accepted on faith. However, Thomas claimed reason is fully competent within its own boundaries and considerations of faith do not need to enter into philosophical arguments. Finally, Thomas believed that the two spheres overlapped somewhat and that some doctrines the humble believer holds on faith (for example, the existence of God) could be proven by the natural light of reason.

Fifth, after Thomas, there was less confidence in the ability of reason to supplement faith. A succession of philosophers progressively narrowed the scope of reason, more and more distancing its relationship to theology. Siger of Brabant, a contemporary of Aquinas, held the doctrine of double truth, which claimed that philosophy could give one answer to a question and theology a different answer. However, Siger made very few attempts to resolve the differences between philosophy and theology. In contrast, Duns Scotus (around 1266–1308) retained the harmony of faith and reason, but allowed for very little overlap between the two. William of Ockham in the fourteenth century was much more extreme. He separated theology and philosophy to protect the truths of faith from the scrutiny of human reason. Claiming that our knowledge of the world yields only probability, he did not think the existence of the biblical God could be proven with any certainty. Furthermore, Ockham separated logic from reality by claiming that it could not tell us about reality but only about the forms of propositions we assert about reality. Finally, the separation of faith and reason was fueled by a vigorous resurgence of mysticism in the fourteenth century that allocated knowledge of God to religious experience and placed it beyond the pale of rational, propositional knowledge.

THE RELATION OF WILL AND INTELLECT

Another Scholastic controversy concerned the relation of the will and intellect. Everyone agreed that certain categories of human actions are good and others are not. The question was, What is the basis of the goodness of these things? One position claimed that God's intellect precedes his will in making decisions. These philosophers believed that the Platonic universals reside in God's mind. By knowing his own mind, God's intellect is aware of those qualities that are objectively good and his will follows this ideal in creating the world. Similarly, those actions that God's intellect discerns are good are what his will commands us to perform. This position followed the assumptions of either extreme or moderate realism, since it said the good is an objective entity. For obvious reasons,

the position is sometimes called **intellectualism**. One practical implication of this view was that since God's intellect recognizes the good, our minds (miniature versions of his intellect) can likewise recognize what is good, and an ethics based on reason is possible. This led to the medieval revival of the Stoic **natural law theory**, which claims that people can discover moral principles by examining human nature.

The second position was known as **voluntarism**. Its advocates claimed that the divine will had priority over the intellect. In this account, it is God's sovereign will that freely chooses what is to be considered good or evil. The voluntarists objected that the intellectualists' position impinges on God's freedom and power, since it implies his will is bound by the prescribed patterns. The extreme voluntarists consistently followed out the logic of this position and claimed that lying or adultery could have been morally good actions had God willed them to be such. It is no more necessary that promise keeping is morally required than it was necessary that God create crocodiles. However, in the world he chose to create, God did make crocodiles and he did will that promises should be kept. Obviously, in this theory the unaided human reason cannot discern what is morally good, since this is a result of God's free and sovereign decision. Ethics necessarily must be based on some sort of revelation of God's moral choices. This is sometimes called the "divine command" ethical theory. The voluntarists tended to be nominalists because they believed that moral goodness is not an eternal universal, but is a "name" that God freely bestows on certain actions. Since our reason cannot discern what is morally good, our wills must simply obey the created moral order revealed in God's commands.

These conflicting positions on the will and intellect also applied to how the Scholastics understood the creation of the world. The intellectualists claimed that creation was preceded by the eternal forms in God's intellect. Although not all subscribed to a strict, logical determinism, they did believe that the outlines of the world were determined by its fittingness to reason. Hence our reason is the best instrument for discovering the world's order. But for voluntarists such as Duns Scotus and Ockham, the world is radically contingent. If God had wanted to, he could have made an entirely different world from the present one, for his will is primary over his intellect. In proposing this view, their motives were primarily religious ones. They wanted to protect the sovereignty and freedom of God and to make necessary a greater reliance on revelation, while giving less authority to reason. But by stressing the contingency of the world, they made observation more important than speculative reasoning in our attempts to understand the world. Eventually, this shift of emphasis was important in nurturing the rise of modern science.

With these key issues as a background, the remainder of the chapter surveys the thought of St. Anselm and Abelard as well as key figures among the medieval Islamic and Jewish philosophers. Anselm illustrates the application of Platonic rationalism and realism to proofs for God's existence. Abelard illustrates the struggle to balance faith and reason and introduces an early version of moral voluntarism. Next, using representative Islamic and Jewish philosophers, the issue of faith and reason is examined again as it applies to the impact of Aristotle's philosophy on their traditional faiths. The European rediscovery of Aristotle is the final topic of this chapter.

St. Anselm

Anselm (1033–1109) was born into Italian nobility. Against his father's wishes, he decided to become a monk at the Benedictine monastery in the Norman town of Bec. Eventually he became the abbot of the monastery. Although he did not think of himself as gifted at administration, others did not share his opinion, and he was summoned to be the Archbishop of Canterbury. He longed to return to the tranquillity of the cloister, but he reluctantly but faithfully served in this position until his death. His sixteen years in this position were filled with controversy because of political tensions between England and Rome. Against two successive kings, he argued the authority of the pope over that of the crown. Anselm died in 1109 at the age of seventy-six and was canonized in 1494.

His philosophical goal was to provide conclusive arguments to rationally demonstrate the Christian teachings he had accepted on faith. With Augustine, he believed that faith necessarily preceded understanding. "I do not seek to understand that I may believe, but I believe in order to understand," Anselm said in the first chapter of his *Proslogium*.[6] Although he was deeply pious, he was also a confident rationalist. Accordingly, he was convinced that all reasoning should follow the deductive method and that this method would lead to all fundamental truths. During Anselm's time, the boundaries between what could be known by reason versus what required revelation had not yet been made clear. Other philosophers had tried to prove such doctrines as the existence of God. However, Anselm's enthusiasm for rationalism led him to believe he could also provide "necessary reasons" for the truth of such doctrines as the Trinity and Incarnation. Later theologians came to recognize that such matters were beyond the competence of reason and had to be established by faith and revelation.

His most famous argument—and the one that ensured him a place in the history of philosophy forever—is the ontological argument for God's existence found in his *Proslogium*.* After many attempts to reason to God's existence, Anselm said the argument "offered itself" to him in a burst of insight that he considered an answer to prayer. The proof depends on the notion that God is a being greater than any that can be conceived. He directs the argument to the "fool" of Psalm 14 who "hath said in his heart, there is no God." Anselm points out that the fool can understand the definition of God, for to deny God requires that you understand what you are denying. Therefore, God exists at least as an idea in the mind or the understanding. The question is, does God exist outside the mind as well? Anselm's argument attempts to show that

---

*The word *ontological* is derived from the Greek and literally means "having to do with the science of being." Thus, this argument attempts to prove God's existence from the concept of his being. The argument was first given this label by the eighteenth-century German philosopher Immanuel Kant.

it is unintelligible to deny this. His argument may be formulated as follows:

(1) I have, within my understanding, an idea of God.

(2) This idea of God is the idea of a being that is the greatest that can be conceived.

(3) A being is greater if it exists in reality than if it exists only in the understanding.

(4) If God (the greatest conceivable being) exists in the understanding alone, then a greater being can be conceived, namely one that also exists in reality.

(5) But premise (4) is a contradiction, for it says I can conceive of a greater being than the greatest conceivable being.

(6) So if I have an idea of the greatest conceivable being, such a being must exist both in my understanding and in reality.

(7) Therefore, God exists in reality.

This argument is based on Plato's conception of reality as described in his account of the Divided Line. In other words, the proof assumes that the greater the perfection of something, the more reality it has. If we can think of the most perfect sort of being, we will, necessarily, be thinking of the being with the greatest degree of reality. Critics of Anselm, both among his contemporaries and in the modern age, have insisted that existence is not a property on the same order as properties such as knowledge, power, or goodness. We can think of a being perfect in every way, but whether that being exists or not is not part of our conception of its perfection.

Anselm provides another version of the argument in *Proslogium*, chapter III. It was not clear to him that this was a completely different argument, for he saw it as merely an elaboration of the first version. However, most philosophers today think that he stumbled on a completely different, and perhaps stronger, line of reasoning. This argument starts out with the same first two premises as the preceding argument, but then takes a different tack. Instead of talking about existence as such, it focuses on the property of necessary existence. A

being whose nonexistence is impossible is one whose existence is necessary. However, a being whose nonexistence is a rationally conceivable possibility is not a necessary being. This version of the proof argues that necessary existence must be attributed to any being that is perfect to the maximum degree. Here is a formulation of Anselm's second argument:

(1) I have an idea of God.

(2) This idea of God is the idea of a being, which is the greatest that can be conceived.

(3) A being whose nonexistence is impossible is greater than a being whose nonexistence is possible.

(4) Thus, if the greatest possible being's nonexistence is rationally conceivable, then he is not the greatest possible being.

(5) But premise (4) is a contradiction.

(6) So the nonexistence of the greatest possible being cannot be rationally conceivable.

(7) Therefore, God necessarily exists.

Premise (3) is based on the principle that the greatest possible being cannot begin to exist and cannot cease to exist, for in either case something else greater than it must cause it to pass into or out of existence. For example, the Empire State Building *happens* to exist, but it could just as easily not have existed. Possibly there is life in outer space, but then again, perhaps not—it all depends on whether or not there are conditions that produced it. So the greatest possible being is one whose existence does not depend on anything else, and this means it must be a being who does not just happen to exist but who exists necessarily. It follows that *if* God exists, he exists necessarily. But Anselm's point is that the word "if" cannot apply to God's existence, for as soon as we say, "If God exists . . ." we are implying that he (like the Empire State Building) conceivably might have not existed. We are stating a contradiction: God is a being whose nonexistence is *possible*, but (by definition) God is a being whose nonexistence is *impossible*. The argument attempts to force us to choose between two alternatives: (1) God exists (and his nonexistence is impossible), or (2) the concept of God is completely meaningless. Thus we must either accept the conclusion or reject the first premise. Certain philosophers in the twentieth century (called *logical positivists*) do maintain that the concept of God is as unintelligible as the concept of a "round square."* However, it seemed clear to Anselm that both theists and atheists are perfectly capable of conceiving of a perfect being such as God. Since we can think of such a being, we cannot suppose his existence is an open question similar to the possibility of life in outer space.

A certain monk named Gaunilo, a contemporary of Anselm, raised a number of objections to the ontological argument in a piece with the witty title "On Behalf of the Fool." He questioned the move from the existence of the greatest conceivable being in the imagination to the existence of such a being in reality. "Isn't it just as easy to imagine the greatest possible island?," Gaunilo asked. If so, must we then conclude, using Anselm's logic, that such an island really exists? The point of this criticism is that Anselm's reasoning would let us rationally prove the actual existence of a wide variety of things (the perfect painting, the perfect steak, the perfect knight), as long as we can imagine that they are the greatest possible member of their species. To summarize Anselm's reply, an island greater than any possible island still would not be a "being than which a greater cannot be conceived." For even the most excellent island is something that, by its nature, is a limited being that has a physical location. Hence, if it exists at location A, it doesn't exist at B. Since we can conceive of it as not existing at B, we can also conceive of it as not existing at all. Thus, he suggests that perfection and necessary existence are qualities that could only be attributed to God.

Gaunilo also attacked premises (1) and (2) of both arguments. Are we really able to fully conceive of a being greater than which none can be conceived? Things we understand, we can understand because we have experiences of them or of things similar to them. However, if the greatest

possible being is singularly unique, then the understanding can only vaguely grope for the significance of these words. Anselm replies that we can compare two things in terms of their different degrees of excellence. From this we can project our notion of a relatively good being to the *n*th degree and conceive of an absolutely good being. To use a contemporary example, we can see that the social reformer Gandhi is morally superior to the Roman tyrant Nero. However, we can imagine someone who has all Gandhi's virtues but none of his human defects. By this same process, the mind can continue on until we conceive of a being who has all possible virtues to the maximum degree with no defects at all. Thus, our human intellects can form the conception of the greatest possible being.

After Anselm, the ontological argument continued to have admirers and critics throughout the history of philosophy. In the modern period, the rationalists Descartes, Spinoza, and Leibniz defended their own versions of the argument. Philosophers who were more oriented toward experience, such as Aquinas and Ockham, among the medieval thinkers, and Kant in the eighteenth century, harshly criticized the argument even though they took the side of theism. Although many do not think it is cogent, philosophers have not been able to lay the argument to rest. As a testimony to the great genius of this eleventh-century monk, his argument is still alive today and is debated using the sophisticated techniques of twentieth-century logic.

Peter Abelard

Peter Abelard (1079–1142) was born near Nantes, France, into a noble Parisian family. He studied at the new schools of philosophy and theology that had grown up at Chartres and Paris. Although admired as an exceptionally brilliant student, he had a reputation for being a disagreeable and arrogant scholar. After completing a course, he often went on to teach the subject himself in competition with his former teacher. This practice tells a lot about his personality, which was not one most people found endearing. He must not have been without some personal charm, however, for when he was thirty-five he fell into a passionate love affair with Héloïse,

*See Chapter 32 on the logical positivists.

the young niece of an official of Notre Dame Cathedral. She became pregnant, and they arranged a secret marriage. For these reasons her uncle was furious at her lover, and in Abelard's own words, her family punished him by "cutting off those parts of my body with which I had done that which was the cause of their sorrow." He retired to the abbey of St. Denis outside of Paris, where he made his profession as a monk, and Héloïse went to a convent to become a nun. His life continued to be haunted by controversy, as his book *On the Divine Unity and the Trinity* was condemned and burned at an ecclesiastical council at Soissons in 1121. Twenty years later, around 1141, he was summoned to a council at Sens and was prosecuted for heresy because of his *Introduction to Theology*. Abelard died in 1142, and when Héloïse died twenty-two years later she was buried at his side.

Abelard is considered a pioneer in using the Aristotelian dialectic to clarify theological propositions. This form of debate came to be the characteristic style of Scholastic discussions. This technique was exhibited in his most famous book, written in 1121–1122, which was titled *Sic et Non* ("Yes and No"). In this work he sets out over 150 theological questions on which the Church Fathers gave conflicting opinions. Contrary to his critics, its purpose was not to produce doubts, but to challenge the minds of students to exercise their intellects by trying to resolve these contradictions. In the Prologue he states, "By doubting we come to questioning, and by questioning we perceive the truth." Abelard's dialectical form of argument was later used by Aquinas with the modification that Aquinas always concluded with his own resolution of the opposing positions. Abelard offended traditionalists because he viewed theology as an opportunity for vigorous debate and questioning rather than for pious meditation and acceptance. Although his theological daring often makes him seem rebellious, he wrote to Héloïse after the condemnation of 1141: "I do not want to be a philosopher if it is necessary to deny Paul. I do not want to be Aristotle if it is necessary to be separated from Christ."[7]

In his discussion of moral problems, Abelard had an important influence on the direction of Scholastic moral theology. He reacted against the legalistic tendencies of his age in which moral goodness was seen simply as an external conformity of an act to the law of God and sin was defined as a factual transgression of law, independent of whether or not the agent knew his action was wrong. Instead, Abelard emphasizes the importance of the intentions and the will of the agent. "God considers not what is done, but in what spirit it is done; and the merit or praise of the agent lies not in the deed, but in the intention." Hence, sin is a contempt for God manifested in our willing what we know to be wrong. But if we act with a sincere conscience and do what we believe is right, we may err, but we do not sin. As theological support for his position, he cites the words of Jesus about his persecutors, "Father, forgive them, for they know not what they do." Abelard's purpose was not to condone simple-minded and ignorant sincerity concerning morality, but to emphasize that the morally good person is one of goodwill who makes a determined effort to know what is good and to act by the best light he or she can find. The fully virtuous act, of course, not only proceeds from the intention to do what is right but also is an act that *is* objectively right, either because it conforms to the natural moral law or to God's specific commands.

Anticipating the position of the fourteenth-century voluntarists, Abelard suggests that there is no necessity to God's moral commands. For this reason, God prescribes different moralities at different times in biblical history. Free choice is basic to God as a lawgiver just as free choice is essential for people to be law followers. But no matter what the material content of the divine law may be, people always have the same formal obligation to obey it.

Abelard was not followed by any distinguishable school of philosophy, but he had a great impact on his time. As we have mentioned previously, his most significant contribution was in his resolution of the controversy over universals. In this, he contributed to the study of how mental concepts are formed and how language functions. Even though most of Aristotle's major works did not become available until later, Abelard anticipated later refinements in philosophy based on these texts. Consequently, he is considered an important contributor to the development of Scholasticism.

Islamic Philosophers

PRESERVING ARISTOTLE'S LEGACY

At a time when the Christian West had but fragments of the works of Plato and Aristotle, Islamic and Jewish philosophers were enjoying the treasures of Greek thought and using them to enrich their speculations. Because of this, Arabian philosophy became one of the main vehicles that carried Aristotle's complete works and later those of Plato to the West. The later Christian medieval scholars were influenced by these Muslim philosophers either by adopting their interpretation of Aristotle or by reacting against their alleged heresies. Similarly, Jewish thinkers of the twelfth century passed on to the West the fruits of their study of Aristotle. Thus, the story of medieval philosophy cannot be told without mentioning the Islamic and Jewish philosophers of this time.

THE RISE OF THE ISLAMIC RELIGION

Islam, which means "submission" (to God's will), is one of the most widespread and powerful monotheistic religions in the world. It is based on the revelations that the prophet Mohammed received over the course of several years. Although he thought his revelations were consistent with those of the Old and New Testaments, he also thought his teachings superseded theirs. His revelations were recorded in the Koran, the holy book of the Islamic religion, and his followers were called Muslims, which means "true believers." The influence of his teachings was so commanding that within a century of Mohammed's death in A.D. 632, his followers had spread Islam to virtually all the inhabited lands from India through North Africa to Spain.

Centuries before the rise of Islam, Christian schools as well as heretical sects in Mesopotamia, Persia, and Syria had kept alive the study of Greek philosophy and science and preserved and translated the ancient texts of Greece. The Islamic religion gave birth to the Islamic philosophical tradition around 800, when Muslim scholars began to translate these Greek works into Arabic and write commentaries on them. The Arab philosophers had an agenda similar to that of the Christian Scholastics, but in this part of the world the task was to reconcile the teachings of Aristotle with the Koran. The history of Islamic philosophy followed the same pattern as the development of Christian philosophy. In both cases a well-established orthodox tradition developed that was based on revealed scriptures (the Koran or the Bible). In both traditions, some philosophers enthusiastically embraced the Greek philosophies and liberally interpreted their scriptures in order to make their faith conform to reason. However, in both cases defenders of a rigid orthodoxy were suspicious of the impact of philosophy on traditional understandings of the faith. Just as the Christian medieval scholars were influenced by Neoplatonism, partly due to the mistaken identity of the Pseudo-Dionysian text, the same sort of confusion occurred in the Arab world. For example, some of the *Enneads* of Plotinus were translated under the title "Aristotle's Theology." Similarly, the *Book of Causes*, taken from the works of the Athenian Neoplatonist Proclus, were attributed to Aristotle. These textual mistakes helped to promote a Neoplatonic interpretation of Aristotle among Islamic philosophers. The Islamic philosophers fell into two groups, an earlier, eastern group in Baghdad, and a later, western group centered in Spain.

AVICENNA

Avicenna (the Latinized name for Ibn Sīnā; 980–1037) was one of the more important Islamic philosophers. Born in Persia, he was a child prodigy, and learned all the disciplines and great works of literature as a young boy. At age sixteen he knew enough to become a physician. Avicenna spent a busy life practicing medicine and serving as a high government official, while still finding time to pursue his scholarship. Even while traveling a great deal, he wrote 160 books, covering a wide range of topics.

Avicenna tells us he memorized Aristotle's *Metaphysics* by reading it forty times but did not understand it until he read Al-Farabi (died 950), a founder of the Aristotelian tradition among the Muslims. His system was based on Al-Farabi's ideas and a Neoplatonic reading of Aristotle. In developing his metaphysics, Avicenna (like Anselm) argues that God's essence necessarily implies his existence. For every other creature in the world, however, their essence and their existence are two different things. For example, the essence of a unicorn is to be a one-horned, horselike mammal. However, from a description of its properties, we cannot determine whether or not a unicorn exists. Yet if all creatures in themselves are merely possible beings, how do some become actual? Obviously, their existence had to be caused by some other existing being. But this series of causes, which are themselves dependent beings, cannot go on indefinitely. Some necessary being must have originally caused mere possibilities to become actualities. This necessary being, of course, is God. This way of reasoning about necessity and possibility influenced both Jewish and Christian thinkers alike, particularly Maimonides and St. Thomas.

From this rather orthodox starting point, however, Avicenna reasons to a very controversial conclusion. Since God is necessary and without a beginning, Avicenna supposed that this implies that all God's attributes are necessary and without a beginning as well, including God's status as the creator of the world. Revealing his Neoplatonic influences, Avicenna develops the theory that the world and everything in it emanates from God out of rational necessity. Thus God was not free in creating the world, for the divine creativity is a necessary feature of his being. Furthermore, if God and all his attributes are eternal, then his creation of the world must have occurred from all eternity. Hence, the world is eternal, although from all eternity it has depended on and emanated from God. Even though no creature exists necessarily in itself, every creature is a necessary feature of a world system that could not be other-

wise than it is. Thus, everything is a part of a logically determined chain of causes. Parts of Avicenna's writings were translated into Latin in the twelfth century, and many Christian thinkers were impressed by the logically rigorous system they provided.

AL-GHAZALI

Al-Ghazali (1058–1111) was a Persian philosopher who could be considered the Islamic counterpart of those voices in Christendom that feared Greek philosophy would corrupt the purity of their faith. In his autobiography, called *Deliverance from Error,* he complained that the problem of philosophical movements is that "the defect of unbelief affects them all." His most influential book was *The Destruction of the Philosophers.** In it, he presents his case against Avicenna and others like him with the passion of a religious fundamentalist along with the intellectual rigor of an accomplished logician. He claimed that the philosophers contradict the Koran, each other, as well as themselves. He considered logic a useful tool as long as it does not make us arrogant. However, logic cannot prove anything in metaphysics and attempting to do so causes unbelief to flourish. He believed philosophical writings should be kept out of the hands of the public, for "just as the poor swimmer must be kept from the slippery banks, so must mankind be kept from reading these books."[8]

The most interesting part of Al-Ghazali's philosophy concerns his analysis of causality. He was disturbed by Avicenna's thesis that the chain of causes and effects flow from God's nature by rational necessity. One consequence of Avicenna's view is that miracles are impossible. A miracle occurs when God causes something to happen that deviates from the normal course of events. But if the system of causes and effects is a rationally necessary whole, then, according to Avicenna's logic, even God could not cause this inevitable pattern

*This is sometimes translated as *The Incoherence of the Philosophers.*

to change. Since orthodox Muslim theology teaches the existence of miracles, Al-Ghazali had to undermine the notion of causality that led to this denial of miracles.

Briefly, he argues that neither logic nor experience can establish any necessary connection between so-called causes and their effects. He uses the example of (X) touching a flame to a piece of cotton and (Y) the combustion of the cotton. True, it would violate our expectations to say the flame touched the cotton but the cotton did not burn. However, although conflicting with our past experience, the occurrence of X but not Y would not contradict the laws of logic. Furthermore, a thousand observations of the flame touching the cotton being followed by the combustion of the cotton could only tell us these two events happened simultaneously in the past. These observations could not show us it is logically necessary that the two events will occur together next time. According to Al-Ghazali, there is no other cause but God. Therefore, the "laws of nature" are not causes but simply describe the way God usually makes things happen. However, God can cause any event to be followed by any other event he wills. It follows that a miraculous deviation from the normal sequence of events is logically possible for God.

Al-Ghazali's arguments concerning causality are similar to those of Nicolas Malebranche (1638–1715) and David Hume (1711–1776). Malebranche, like Al-Ghazali, used this sort of argument to support his theism. Hume, however, was not interested in divine causality. Instead, he used a similar analysis of causality to support the skeptical conclusion that causal judgments do not have a logical foundation.

AVERROËS

Averroës (Ibn Rushd; 1126–1198) of Cordova was the most outstanding Muslim philosopher in Spain. He came from a family of prominent judges and served for many years as a judge himself. He also achieved prominence as a physician, astronomer, and philosopher. He is best known for his three sets of commentaries on Aristotle. The influence of these works were so great that the medieval Christian scholars referred to him simply as "the Commentator."

He responded to Al-Ghazali's *Destruction of the Philosophers* by writing a point-by-point refutation of it in a work titled *The Destruction of the Destruction*. In other works he defended the thesis that Aristotle represents the culmination of the human intellect and argued that his philosophy did not conflict with the Koran. He points out that the Koran presents the world as God's handiwork and concludes that this lets us demonstrate God's existence and nature by studying the world. Aristotle's logic, physics, and metaphysics provide us with the tools for such a demonstration, and Averroës cites Aristotle's argument for an Unmoved Mover as an example.

His most famous device for reconciling theology and philosophy is his so-called double-truth theory. He theorizes that the Koran was written for the masses, who do not have great powers of the intellect. For this reason, it was written in an allegorical style to appeal to the emotions and the imagination of the uneducated. Consequently, the philosopher must strip away the surface meaning to uncover the true or "inner meaning." Although the conclusions of philosophical reasoning may seem to conflict with religious tradition, this is only a conflict with the apparent meaning of the scriptures. In the final analysis, truth cannot conflict with truth, so the best of philosophy is consistent with the hidden meaning of the Koran.

Averroës' position was badly misinterpreted by thirteenth-century Christians who opposed him as well as by those who admired him. They mistakenly thought Averroës was saying that some proposition X could be literally true in philosophy while its contradictory, *Not-X*, could be literally true in religion. The faculty at the newly founded University of Paris seemed to enthusiastically endorse this mistaken interpretation in their attempts to adopt Averroës' explication of Aristotle. This group, known as the "Latin Averroists" was headed by Siger of Brabant (about 1240–1284). To embrace many Aristotelian doctrines that were contrary to Church teachings, they tended to shuffle philosophy and theology into separate compartments without any attempt to relate the two. As opposed to this extreme double-truth theory, Averroës was actually saying the truth could be expressed at different levels and in different ways, figuratively in religion and literally in philosophy. Apart from the misinterpretations imposed on him, what is revolutionary about Averroës is that this method of interpretation implies that theology yields its authority to philosophy: the philosopher decides how revelation should be interpreted to make it consistent with philosophical reason.

Averroës' quarrel with the traditionalists led to his disfavor, and his books were burned in Islamic Spain. To prevent any further outbreaks of heresy, a general suppression of Greek philosophy was instituted. Fourteen years after the death of Averroës, the Muslim culture in Spain suffered its own downfall. In 1212, Christian forces defeated a Muslim army at Las Navas de Tolsa, breaking the Muslim hold over Spain. By the close of this century, the Christian reconquest of Spain was complete, except for the region of Grenada, which remained Muslim until 1492. As Western Christendom expanded into Muslim Spain, the works of Averroës found their way into the European universities. By 1250 Latin translations of his Aristotelian commentaries began to make a sensation in Christendom. The effect of Averroës on Christian thought was twofold. On the one hand, his interpretation of Aristotle purged some of the Neoplatonic distortions added by earlier commentaries. His insights on Aristotle's texts were so respected by Christian scholars that, as noted, he was called "the Commentator" by late medieval philosophers. On the other hand, the heretical elements in his philosophy—such as his determinism, the claim that the world is eternal, and his apparent rejection of personal immortality—cast suspicions on any attempts to merge Aristotle with Christian thought. Although Thomas Aquinas seemed to have learned much from his Islamic predecessor, he also labored long and hard to show that Aristotle's thought did not lead to Averroës' heresies. Nevertheless, because of their common link to Aristotle, Aquinas became tainted with Averroism in the minds of many of his critics.

Jewish Philosophers

Like the Islamic thinkers, the Jewish philosophers were concerned to reconcile their conclusions with an orthodox interpretation of their faith. For the Jewish thinkers, this meant developing a philosophical system based on the Old Testament and the Talmud, an enormous commentary on the first five books of the Bible. The greatest medieval Jewish philosopher was Moses Maimonides (1135–1204), who was born at Cordova, in Spain. He was confident of the harmony between faith and reason. He said his *Guide for the Perplexed* was written for those who have studied philosophy and are confused as to how to harmonize it with the faith. If there is an apparent conflict between an airtight philosophical demonstration and the statements in the Old Testament, Maimonides taught that we should interpret the Scriptures allegorically. Although he believed Aristotle had attained the highest in human knowledge, he recognized a genuine conflict between Aristotle's belief in the eternity of the world on the one hand, and revelation on the other, for Scripture makes it clear that the world had a beginning. Maimonides' solution was to show that Aristotle's arguments are not conclusive and need not be accepted. However, despite his attempts to remain faithful to the Talmud in appropriating Aristotle's insights, conservative Jewish scholars branded him a heretic. His purely theological writings were accepted as authoritative, but his philosophical works were condemned and neglected by Jewish scholars until the nineteenth century.

Because of persecution, the European Jewish community became more isolated from the mainstream of society. This benefited their conservative religious leaders, who wished to purge the community of scientific and secular influences. For many centuries, both Judaism and Islam allowed only mysticism to remain as a supplementary source of knowledge to revelation. Thus, after 1200, only the Christian West could take advantage of Aristotle's insights in developing a comprehensive intellectual system. Because of his groundbreaking work in constructing a biblical Aristotelian philosophy, however, Maimonides greatly influenced Christian scholars, especially Aquinas.

The Rediscovery of Aristotle in Europe

In the latter part of the twelfth century, a new world opened up for European thinkers. Greek works on mathematics, astronomy, medicine, and, most importantly, the complete works of Aristotle became available for the first time. Furthermore, some of the latter's Greek commentators as well as the Arabic and Jewish philosophers were being translated into Latin and becoming known. Between 1210 and 1225 nearly all the works of Aristotle had been translated from the Arabic and were beginning to make waves in Western Christendom. The Church met Aristotle's philosophy with a great deal of suspicion, mainly because of the pantheistic accretions that the Arabs had added to it. The necessity and eternity of the world as well as the blurring of the distinction between the creator and creation were doctrines unacceptable to the Christian West. In 1215, the statutes of the University of Paris announced that the study of Aristotle's *Physics* and *Metaphysics* was forbidden. However, this proved ineffective, for scholars continued to study these works and write commentaries on them. Later in the century, scholars in the West began to translate the major works from the original Greek. In consequence, a picture of the authentic Aristotle began to emerge, freed of any pantheistic distortions. By 1254 the *Physics* and the *Metaphysics* were considered so important that they entered the curriculum of the University of Paris. Scholars began to frame their questions in philosophical terms such as the distinction between essence and existence, the difference between necessary and contingent being, and Aristotle's theory of abstraction. With the influx of new philosophical models, the question now had to be asked, can these non-Christian philosophical systems, which came from pagan Greece, Islam, and Judaism, be converted to Christian thought, or

should the Christian world avoid them? This question set the agenda for the thirteenth century, when Thomas Aquinas would provide a history-making answer.

Questions for Understanding

1. What factors were responsible for the return to philosophy in the eleventh and twelfth centuries?

2. What was the goal of Scholasticism?

3. What is the problem of universals in the medieval period? In what ways did theological considerations enter into this controversy?

4. What were the various positions taken on the problem of universals, and who were some proponents of each position?

5. What were the various positions taken on the problem of faith and reason during this period, and what were the names of some figures associated with each position?

6. What was the problem of the relationship between the will and the intellect during this period? What were the two major positions in this debate?

7. What was Anselm's ontological argument? In what ways do the two versions of it differ?

8. How did Gaunilo attempt to refute Anselm's argument?

9. What were the key features of Abelard's philosophy?

10. In what ways were the debates within medieval Islamic philosophy similar to those of their Christian counterparts?

11. How did Avicenna attempt to argue for the existence of God?

12. Why does Avicenna believe that the way that the world was created was rationally necessary?

13. What was Al-Ghazali's view of philosophy?

14. How does Al-Ghazali's analysis of causality provide an argument for the possibility of miracles?

15. According to Averroës, what is the relationship between Aristotle's philosophy and the Islamic faith?

16. How does Averroës use his double-truth theory to reconcile faith and reason?

17. Who was the greatest medieval Jewish philosopher? How does he attempt to reconcile faith and reason?

18. In the latter part of the twelfth century, Aristotle's philosophy was rediscovered in Christian Europe. What were some of the effects of this development?

Questions for Reflection

1. Concerning the relationship between faith and reason, Peter Damian and St. Bernard of Clairvaux thought that faith and reason were opposed, whereas Thomas Aquinas thought that reason could supplement faith. Pretend that you are a medieval Christian thinker and construct a defense of one or the other position.

2. In the Middle Ages, the two positions on the will and the intellect were intellectualism and voluntarism. Given the theological assumptions of these thinkers, what arguments did defenders of each view give for their position? What difficulties could opponents point to in each position?

3. Do you think that Anselm's ontological argument is sound? Which premise do you think is the most controversial? Write a short essay either defending or criticizing this premise.

4. What do you think of Al-Ghazali's analysis of causality? Write a brief defense or critique of his view.

Notes

1. Boethius, *Commentary on Porphyry's Introduction*, trans. Richard McKeon, in *Selections from Medieval Philosophers*, vol. 1, ed. Richard McKeon (New York: Scribner's, 1929), 91.

2. *The Glosses of Peter Abelard on Porphyry*, in *Selections from Medieval Philosophers*, vol. 1, ed. Richard McKeon (New York: Scribner's, 1929), 240.

3. *On Divine Omnipotence* (Epist. 2.17), trans. Owen J. Blum in *Medieval Philosophy: From St. Augustine to Nicholas of Cusa*, ed. John F. Wippel and Allan B. Wolter (New York: Macmillan, Free Press, 1969), 150–151.

4. Sermon 76, quoted in A. C. McGiffert, *A History of Christian Thought*, vol. 2 (New York: Scribner's, 1933), 226.

5. *De Fide Trinitatis*, quoted in McGiffert, 186.

6. *Proslogium*, chap. 1, in *Saint Anselm: Basic Writings*, trans. S. N. Deane (La Salle, IL: Open Court, 1962).

7. *Epistola 17*, quoted in Armand A. Maurer, *Medieval Philosophy* (New York: Random House, 1962), 59–60.

8. *Deliverance from Error*, 3.2, quoted in James N. Jordan, *Western Philosophy: From Antiquity to the Middle Ages* (New York: Macmillan, 1987), 350.

11

St. Thomas Aquinas: Aristotle's Philosophy and Christian Thought

The Ox That Roared

Thomas Aquinas was born in 1225 (some say 1224) into a noble Italian family who lived in southern Italy about halfway between Rome and Naples. His father was the Count of Aquino, a man prominent in politics. Thomas was groomed by his family for a career of service in the Church. However, his parents' motives were not as pious as they may seem. They had always dreamed that Thomas would rise to a position of ecclesiastical authority where he would be politically influential and even wealthy. Around age fourteen he was sent to the University of Naples. It was an exciting place to be, abounding in new ideas, partly because the recently discovered Aristotelian texts and their Arabian commentaries had become a prominent part of the curriculum. Thomas came under the influence of the newly formed Dominican Order, which he joined sometime around 1244.

So it might seem that his parents' plans were proceeding nicely. They were not pleased, however, for the Dominicans did not aspire to be influential administrators but were humble and impoverished preachers and scholars. To bring Thomas to his senses, while he was en route to Paris his brothers kidnaped him and locked him in a tower for over a year. Eventually, his family realized the seriousness of his commitment and let him go on to his life's mission.

He picked up his life where it had been interrupted and went to Paris to study philosophy and theology, where he came under the influence of the Dominican theologian Albert the Great.* Aquinas was a very large, rotund person, whose imposing frame was contrasted with his gentle personality. In his classes he quietly absorbed the material without entering into the vigorous discussions of his classmates, who consequently ridiculed him as "the dumb ox." Albert, with keen insight into Thomas's intellectual potential, scolded them saying, "I tell you, the bellows of this 'dumb ox' will awaken all of Christendom." There is a story about Thomas that, although

---

*This name was not a reference to either his fame or his bulk, but was a translation of his German name of Albrecht Gross.

historically questionable, rings true to what we know of his sincere personality. One day, the brothers in the monastery conspired to play a practical joke on poor Brother Thomas. When he came into the room, one of them exclaimed that there was a cow flying in the sky. Thomas slowly ambled over to the window to see it, whereon the monks roared with laughter, asking, "Brother Thomas, did you really think that a cow could fly?" Thomas quietly replied, "I would much rather believe that a cow could fly, than that a brother monk would lie to me."

After earning the highest degree in theology, Aquinas spent the remainder of his life lecturing and writing while alternately residing in Paris and Italy, as well as making frequent journeys to conduct the business of his order and the Church. He was appointed by the Pope to be a theological adviser in conversations with leaders of the Eastern Orthodox Church. Aquinas died at age forty-nine, in 1274, on his way to attend the Council of Lyons to carry out this diplomatic mission.

Aquinas was an astoundingly prolific writer—his works fill some twenty-five volumes. He is said to have kept four secretaries busy at once, dictating different manuscripts in progress to them, which they would then transcribe. His works run the gamut from devotional works, sermons, lectures, technical works in philosophy and theology, as well as commentaries on Aristotle, Boethius, and Pseudo-Dionysius. The *Summa Theologica*, his major work, is longer than the entire collected works of Aristotle. All this was accomplished in the last twenty years of his life while teaching and consulting. While celebrating Mass a few months before he died, he had a mystical experience. "I can write no more," he later said to a friend, "I have seen things which make all my writings like straw." Without any further explanation, he gave up writing. In 1323, within a half-century of his death, he was canonized by the Church, which means he was officially declared a saint. In 1879 Pope Leo XIII recommended the philosophy of Thomas Aquinas as a model for Catholic thought.

Aquinas's Task: Integrating Philosophy and Faith

THE IMPACT OF ARISTOTLE

A dramatic shift in European medieval philosophy began to occur in the twelfth and thirteenth centuries as Aristotle's complete works began to be made widely available. Aristotle was very attractive to anyone who read him seriously, for he offered the most powerful and comprehensive system the medieval world had ever seen. However, his newly discovered works brought with them not only new perspectives, but new problems as well. The main difficulty was that while many found Aristotle's arguments persuasive, a number of his teachings seemed to contradict Christian doctrine. For example, Aristotle taught that the world was eternal and uncreated, and he seemed to deny personal immortality. The Christians who followed Averroes' interpretation of Aristotle tended to modify traditional theology to fit the outlines of their rational systems. Obviously, this caused the Church authorities to be suspicious of Christian philosophers who attempted to make use of the pagan Greek philosophy of Aristotle.* In addition to the problems in Aristotle's teachings, Neoplatonic philosophy had held the minds of Christian thinkers for so long that the empirical and naturalistic perspective of Aristotle seemed alien and dangerous.

Contrary to the fears of the Church authorities, Aquinas believed that adopting Aristotelianism did not necessarily lead to heretical conclusions. He

---

*Aristotle's works on natural philosophy were banned by the Council of Paris in 1210. Various ecclesiastical authorities issued other bans in 1215, 1245, and 1263. The most important condemnation was pronounced by Etienne Tempier, Bishop of Paris, in 1277, a few years after Aquinas's death. The bishop condemned 219 propositions, threatening excommunication to anyone who embraced them. Most of the banned doctrines were those of the Averroists, but some of them were held by Aquinas. A similar condemnation was issued in Oxford eleven days later and again in 1284 and 1286. Eventually, however, largely because of Aquinas's work, the consensus shifted, and Aristotelian Christianity became accepted.

was convinced that Aristotle could be Christianized and could serve as a rich resource for philosophical and theological speculation faithful to the Christian tradition. Although his teacher, Albert the Great, had made some attempts to use Aristotle in a Christian framework, it was Aquinas who became the chief architect of the new philosophical-theological edifice based on this new foundation.

Platonic Christianity had served the needs of the culture for a time. However, the Platonic emphasis on the eternal and its otherworldly notion of the spiritual realm could not keep pace with the changes occurring in the thirteenth century. Increased travel and the flowering of art, architecture, science, and medicine, as well as the rise of the universities, called for a new look at the relationship between Christianity and culture. What was needed was an understanding of how Christianity could hold onto its concern for a transcendent God, as well as its emphasis on the spiritual realm and the afterlife and yet, at the same time, still speak to our here-and-now earthly concerns. By merging Aristotle with Christian theology, Aquinas thought he could gain a perspective on our human involvement in culture, science, politics, and bodily existence that would be philosophically rigorous and theologically adequate.

Aquinas's deep respect for Aristotle is shown by the fact that he frequently refers to him simply as "the Philosopher." However, Aquinas cannot be accused of a slavish duplication of Aristotle's ideas. Aquinas certainly felt free to criticize his Greek model and to dismiss Aristotle's ideas when they did not seem to conform to reason. Aquinas believed that Aristotle's philosophy was superb as far as it goes. But with respect to the distinctive features of the Christian faith, Aristotle was in the dark, and—like any other pagan Greek—in need of divine revelation.

THE SPHERES OF FAITH AND REASON

As discussed in the previous chapter, a major issue during the Middle Ages was the relationship of faith and reason. Accordingly, one of Aquinas's

primary tasks was to show how these two sources of knowledge fit together. Those in the Augustinian tradition (which would include the Protestant Reformers in the centuries to come) emphasized the damage sin has done to our rational powers. They believed that the mind must be renewed by grace before reason can function correctly. For this reason, they claimed that religious faith was a necessary prerequisite for philosophical understanding and that philosophy must keep its place as the humble servant of theology. Aquinas, however, believed that sin did not decisively affect our rational powers. Sin affects our moral life but not our rational life. Hence, Aquinas believed that reason can stand on its own two feet as an independent and autonomous source of knowledge apart from faith. For Aquinas, the only faith necessary in pursuing philosophical truth is faith in the power of the human intellect and the intelligibility of the universe. Of course, he shared this commitment with most philosophers in the Western tradition, both Christian and non-Christian.

Thomas Aquinas achieved a great compromise between Christian teaching and philosophy by giving each its due and seeking to show that they could coexist peacefully. Unlike most previous medievals, Aquinas clearly separates theology from philosophy. Theology gives us knowledge through faith and revelation, and philosophy gives us knowledge through the natural powers of human cognition available to all. They differ in their methods, and each is self-contained and independent of the other. Thus, for Aquinas, the realm of human knowledge can be divided into two areas: (1) truths given to us in revelation and known by faith and (2) truths revealed in nature and known by reasoning from experience. We can diagram Aquinas's view of the relationship between faith and reason as shown in Figure 11-1. The two approaches to knowledge are complementary because theology starts from God and moves to knowledge of the world, whereas philosophy moves from empirical facts about nature and reasons to God. Line A–B represents Christian teachings that are matters of faith, known only through revelation. They are beyond the scope of reason, yet they are not contrary to reason. Although we can disprove objections to them and dismiss alleged contradictions or difficulties, they can neither be proven nor disproven. For Aquinas, examples of truths that cannot be demonstrated by natural reason are the Trinity, the Incarnation, original sin, the creation of the world in time, the sacraments, and the last judgment.*

Line C–D represents knowledge based on sensory experience and the self-evident rational principles of philosophy (such as Aristotle's laws of logic). These scientific and philosophical truths cannot be known through revelation. To give an example of Aquinas's point, to understand the biological functions of the heart we must do empirical research on that organ and cannot simply study the word "heart" as it is used in the Bible.

Finally, line B–C is where revelation overlaps with philosophical knowledge. We can approach these truths either from the side of faith or from the side of reason. The existence of God, his essential attributes, the existence of the soul, immortality, and the details of the natural moral law are examples of truths that can be grounded either in faith or proven by reason.

Thus for Aquinas there are two kinds of theology: (1) revealed or supernatural theology (represented by line A–C on the diagram on p. 171) and (2) **natural theology** or theology not based on revelation (line B–C). Natural theology is that discipline within philosophy that seeks to prove conclusions about God based on our natural reason and experience. Where they overlap, theology and philosophy cannot conflict because both reveal truths that have their origin in the Author of all truth. What can conflict are human interpretations or judgments of either. True theology

is only contradicted by false philosophy, and true philosophy conflicts only with false theology.

METHOD

Thomas Aquinas's best-known work is his *Summa Theologica*, a formidable example of natural theology. In this work and others, Aquinas's method of argument is a paradigm of intellectual rigor and follows the technique of dialectic that was refined by Abelard. Aquinas's discussion of each individual issue systematically proceeds through five steps. First, he states the question at issue. Second, he lists numerous "objections." These are standard answers to the question that he considers incorrect but for which some authority can be cited. In doing this, he tries to state his opponents' positions as strongly and fairly as possible. The third section begins with the words "On the contrary. . . ." Here, he provides an answer to the question that contradicts the previous ones but that supports his own views and for which a counterauthority can be cited, such as Scripture or a noted theologian. The fourth and main section begins with "I answer that . . . ," and he goes on to develop his own view and arguments in its defense. Finally, in the fifth section, he details a series of separate replies to each of the objections originally offered against his position. He proceeds in this way, issue after issue, in his attempt to give an exhaustive and definitive treatment of every major question. In doing this he shows that he is conversant with the history of philosophy from the pre-Socratics to the end of Greek philosophy, as well as the Church Fathers and theologians and the leading Arab and Jewish thinkers. No one fails to get his attention as he shows where his predecessors were illuminating and where their reasoning went astray. The structure of each individual issue in the *Summa Theologica* is matched by the tightly crafted structure of the whole work. Some have said that Thomas Aquinas succeeded in constructing a cathedral of reason that rivaled the great feats of architecture of his time. Using Aristotelian logic, his arguments build on one another and produce a philosophical edifice that leads the

---

*Aquinas differs on these points from many of his predecessors and contemporaries. To various degrees, Augustine, Anselm, and Abelard thought that natural reason pointed to the doctrine of the Trinity. Bonaventure (1221–1274) thought that the creation of the world in time was philosophically provable. Finally, Anselm believed that the Incarnation could be shown to be philosophically necessary.

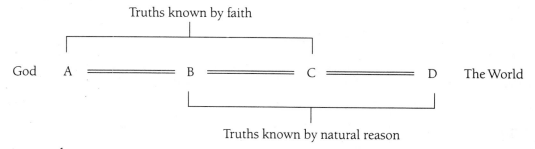

FIGURE 11-1 Thomas Aquinas's view of faith and reason

The Nature of Knowledge: Reason Processing Experience

Thomas Aquinas's epistemology reflects the empirical emphasis of Aristotle. Quoting Aristotle, he says that prior to experience the mind is like a blank tablet (ST 1.79.2).[1] Hence, unlike the Platonist theologians, Aquinas does not believe there is any innate knowledge. Even the idea of God is not written on the mind. However, even though the senses provide the intellect with its content, sensory cognition is not enough to explain our knowledge. "Although the operation of the intellect has its origin in the senses, yet, in the thing apprehended through the senses, the intellect knows many things which the senses cannot perceive" (ST 1.78.4).

The intellect is both passive and active. As passive, it receives its raw materials from sense experience. However, in sense experience we are not bombarded with a meaningless, random confusion of isolated sense data. Because the objects of experience are created entities, they are intelligible and contain forms or universals. However, the active part of the intellect must process sense experience in order to recognize the universals within particular objects. For example, the eyes can show us red things, but reason can isolate the universal of redness. The active intellect, then, functions by abstracting the universals from particulars. Even though the human mind is originally contentless, its nature is such that it has the potential to receive the forms (unlike animals). It is important to note that for Aquinas (unlike Augustine) this is a self-sufficient, natural process that does not need special divine illumination to obtain universal knowledge.

Aquinas could be characterized as a moderate realist. Unlike the extreme realists, he did not believe universals were completely independent realities. The only realities in the world are concrete particulars, and universals exist within particulars. Yet, unlike the nominalists, he did not believe universals are only mental creations. When the mind abstracts universals from objects, it is dealing with real features of the world and not arbitrary categories. For Aquinas, universals first existed from all eternity as ideas within the divine mind. With creation, universals came to exist extramentally in individual substances as their form. Finally, universals exist in the minds of rational creatures when they come to have rational knowledge of particulars through intellectual abstraction.

Given his empiricist starting point, Aquinas has set himself quite a challenge, for he must show that all the intellectual concepts of philosophy and knowledge of spiritual realities such as

intellect to its Maker. Thus, the architecture of both the medieval cathedral and Aquinas's philosophical system were intended to reflect the tightly woven, purposeful hierarchical structure of the universe itself.

God and values somehow derive from the materials of the senses. A further implication of his epistemology, which will become clear in later sections, is that all our knowledge about the world, whether of God, universals, or values, is inferential and indirect.

Metaphysics: From the World to God

THE PHYSICAL WORLD

If we were to follow Aquinas's order of exposition in the *Summa Theologica*, we would begin with his proofs for the existence of God and then go on to consider the created world. However, a number of features of his discussion of God rely on certain principles about the nature of reality that seemed more obvious to his contemporaries than they may to the modern reader. Hence, it will be worthwhile to begin with an overview of his general metaphysical scheme and then see how his conclusions about God fit into this.

Following Aristotle, Aquinas believes that the natural world consists of a collection of concrete individual substances (Lassie the Dog, Socrates the philosopher, the oak tree outside my office, the Hope diamond). Every material substance must be understood in terms of two principles. The first is the substantial form. The form is the universal aspect of the thing, that which all members of a species have in common. The substantial form of humanity, for example, is what gives humans those attributes (physical and mental) that differentiate them from plants and animals, and it is this form that causes them to act in characteristically human ways.

The other aspect of a substance is its matter. We might be inclined to think that the matter of a tree is the woody, fibrous material we associate with the interior of the tree. However, this matter is already the product of the substantial form, and thus it does not exist apart from the substance of the tree. Aquinas's theory of matter attempts to solve two problems that arise from our commonsense understanding of experience. The first one is the problem

of continuity. Since one kind of substance can change into another substance (the tree can be burned and reduced to ashes), what accounts for our experience of continuity? The second problem is that of individuation. How can two substances have *identical* qualities (such as two identical vases) and still be two *different* substances?

To solve the first problem, Aquinas says that if there is continuity, there must be a more fundamental kind of matter that persists through any sort of substantial change. If the tree turns into ashes, then there must be something that had the potential to be the wood of the tree *as well as* the matter of the ashes. This is what Aquinas calls *prime matter*. It is pure matter, without any form whatsoever, and thus it does not have any distinctive characteristics of its own, but has the potential to take on any possible form. It may be described as "pure potentiality." Postulating prime matter also solves the problem of individuation. Two substances with the same qualities are different because their matter is different. However, when we look about the world, we will not find any examples of prime matter. This is because all matter we encounter is already formed matter and is found only in this or that particular substance, whether it is a rock, a plant, or an animal. Of course, in Aquinas's Aristotelian universe there are no pure, independently existing forms either, for all forms are only found embodied in substances.

A HIERARCHICAL UNIVERSE

The distinction between form and matter in physical substances is one example of a more general distinction between *actuality* and *potentiality*. We have said that prime matter is pure potentiality. It is the capacity to take on different substantial forms. Forms are on the side of actuality, for they create a particular tree, tiger, or person. Because God is perfect, he alone is fully actualized, for to be imperfect means to have potentialities that are not actualized. Hence, God cannot change. However, the rest of the universe is dynamic. Every created being is somewhere between pure potentiality and complete actualization and has a natural tendency toward further self-development. In trying to fulfill our potential and be all that we can be, we are imitating or coming closer (within the bounds of our finiteness) to the fullness of the divine actuality and perfection.

Aquinas's picture of the universe is of a continuous hierarchy that some have called the "great chain of being." It ranges from inorganic substances at the bottom all the way up to God at the pinnacle. There is such an enormous variety of substances because God's own creation was made to express his fullness. Aquinas even uses this notion to prove the existence of angels. They are like God in that they are purely spiritual beings, yet they are like humans in that they have potentiality. Thus they fill a unique niche in the chain of being. Although Aquinas did not wrestle with issues of ecology, it is clear that on his view, the disappearance of a species would be unfortunate, for it would leave a gap in nature.

Whether or not we accept Aquinas's Aristotelian view of the world, such a metaphysic offers a great deal of intellectual satisfaction because it assures us that the world is not a meaningless and random hodgepodge of blind processes. Since each species has a form, the world is orderly and intelligible and our minds can know it. Furthermore, the world is purposeful, for each sort of thing is in the process of fulfilling its divinely ordained essence. Also, objective value judgments (such as "better" or "worse") are possible because the excellence of any natural creature can be graded in terms of how fully it realizes the potential inherent in its essence. Finally, creatures can be ranked as higher or lower depending on how close they are to God on the scale of being. Because there is this objective hierarchy, we would save the life of a human being before that of a snail. This is because humans are higher than the animals and just a little lower than the angels. All of physical nature reflects the divine nature and is important, but humans more fully exhibit the image of God and, thereby, have more dignity and worth.

ESSENCE AND EXISTENCE

The potentiality–actuality distinction is exhibited in another distinction, the relation between *essence* and *existence*. **Essence** accounts for what a thing is. It is what is described in dictionary definitions. However, (1) the nature or essence of something differs from (2) the fact that it exists. We could describe to a child the respective properties of kangaroos and unicorns. She would then understand the essence of each kind of creature, but this knowledge alone would not tell her that one of these creatures exists and the other doesn't. So, with respect to all finite beings, their essence is something independent of their existence. But this distinction is not present in God, for God's essence implies his existence. God is a being so great nothing greater can be thought. Such a being could not pass out of existence, as did the dinosaurs, nor could he just happen to exist, as do kangaroos. Hence, if there is a God, his nature is such that he would exist *necessarily*.

This sounds very much like Anselm's ontological argument. However, Aquinas rejects this argument because even though we can understand the term "God" we do not have a direct apprehension of the divine essence. If we did, we would see that his essence is identical to his existence. However, lacking this complete knowledge of the divine essence, we cannot argue from it to God's actual existence as Anselm tries to do. This is consistent with Aquinas's epistemology, for he continually insists that reason must work from the materials given to it by sense experience. Hence, as we will see in the next section, any arguments for God's existence must, necessarily, begin with human experience of the world.

THE EXISTENCE OF GOD

Aquinas presents us with five arguments for the existence of God (using his own words, these are commonly referred to as "the five ways") (ST 1.2.3). He claims no originality for these proofs, since he draws on arguments proposed by Aristotle and some of the latter's Arab and Jewish commentators. However, Aquinas articulates and packages these arguments so artfully that they have become the model for theistic proofs throughout the centuries. Every one of the five ways has this general outline:

(1) If the world has feature X, then there is a God.

(2) The world has feature X.

(3) Therefore, there is a God.

In each of the arguments, he claims that the feature of the world being focused on is one that cannot be explained on the basis of the finite, natural world alone. Hence, Aquinas is drawing our attention to five facts about the world that he believes point to the existence of God. The first three arguments are similar, in that they depend on the principle that an infinite regress of causes is inconceivable. These three "ways" to God are various forms of what is known in modern times as the **cosmological argument**.

The first proof starts from the fact that motion occurs in the world. "Motion" here is understood in the broad Aristotelian sense of any change from a potential state to an actual state. This not only includes changes in location but also refers to, say, a change in temperature or color. He argues that any change presupposes some agent that brings it about. But if the agent is itself a changing being, it too can be moved only by the action of some other agent. However, such a series of agents cannot be infinite. The whole process of things actualizing the potential in other things needs some ultimate ground. Hence, there must be a first Unmoved Mover—a being that is not itself changing but is the ultimate source of the series of changes we observe in the world. To illustrate this point, we can imagine a set of pool balls sitting on a table, racked up in a triangular formation. Although those balls have the potential to move, they will sit there motionless, for all eternity, unless some agent intervenes within the system to set them in motion. If we walked into a room where they *were* in motion and saw the cue ball hitting the number 3 ball, which in turn set the number 10 ball in motion, and even if no one was currently visible, we would still know that *someone or something* had been there to introduce motion into the system. Once the cue ball is in motion, it can impart its motion to others, but the system by itself cannot actualize its own potential for motion. Even if the balls had been in motion continuously from all eternity, they would still need a cause of their eternal motion.

How can something cause motion without itself moving? Here, Aquinas is relying on Aristotle's notion that it is possible for one thing to move another without the cause itself being in motion. For example, you can be madly in love with someone and that love can affect your behavior, but (unfortunately) the object of your love may be unmoved by you in turn (ST 1.105.2). Consequently, the person that causes a response in you is an "unmoved mover."

The second way is an argument from efficient causation. In nature we see that one event is caused by another event that was itself caused by yet another event. There cannot be an infinite series of such causes, because unless there is a first cause that is sufficient unto itself, the whole series of dependent causes and effects is unaccounted for. To illustrate, imagine a long chain hanging in the air. There is no problem in explaining the cause of link 1 being suspended, because we can see that it is supported by link 2, and this one, in turn, is supported by link 3, and so on. However, at some point the entire series of links must be supported by something that does not depend for its support on something else. Without a self-supporting point on which the whole chain depends, the entire chain will never be supported. This First Cause for all the intermediate causes in the world is God.

The third way shifts the emphasis a little and proceeds from the notions of possibility and necessity. This argument takes the following form:

(1) In nature we find things that come into existence and pass out of existence. (Their existence and non-existence are both possible.)

(2) That which does not exist can only begin to exist through something that already has existence.

(3) There cannot be an infinity of merely possible beings who depend for their existence on something else.

(4) Therefore, there must be some being who exists by its own necessity and is not dependent on anything but who can impart existence to everything else.

(5) This necessary being is what all people speak of as God.

To illustrate Aquinas's point, imagine a series of mirrors in a dark room. It is possible for the mirrors to reflect light, but this possibility must be actualized. Now let us suppose that mirror 1 is reflecting light. Where did it come from? Let's say it is receiving light that is being reflected off the surface of mirror 2. But what is the cause of its light? It has received light that was being reflected off of mirror 3, and so on. In the case of any particular mirror, we may be able to account for its light by finding its source in some other mirror. However, this process cannot go on forever. Since mirrors cannot generate their own light, the fact that any one of them is reflecting light must mean that light entered the system from some source outside the system that did not need to receive its light from another (such as a flashlight). Even if we postulate an infinite number of mirrors, each reflecting another's light, this will not solve the problem if none of these mirrors produce their own light. Furthermore, there must be more than just an original source of light at the beginning. Unless some *continuous* source of light sustains the activity of the mirrors' reflection of light, the whole system will lapse back into darkness. Just as the flashlight accounts for its own light and can in turn provide it to others, so there must be a necessary being whose essence it is to exist and who can provide existence to others.

Notice that this argument is similar to Anselm's ontological argument in that they both conclude that a necessary being exists, which is God. However, they differ in that Aquinas arrived at this conclusion through experience and not from the concept of God alone. Notice also that in each of these first three arguments, one particular event (whether a case of motion or change, a given effect, or the bringing of a possible being into existence) can be explained by another neighboring event within the system. However, if we want an ultimate explanation of how the entire series of events could exist at all, we must go outside the system to an entirely different type of reality. So far, these first three arguments establish the existence of an ultimate cause. However, Aristotle used similar arguments to defend the existence of his impersonal divinity. Thus, Aquinas's final two proofs

help round out the picture of the Unmoved Mover by introducing elements that do more to suggest the presence of personality.

The fourth way focuses on degrees of perfection. It starts from the existence of degrees of value or perfection and claims that they imply the existence of a supremely perfect being as their source. When we see the cool, soft light of the moon, we realize that it is caused by, and is a diminished reflection of, the brilliant, blazing light of the sun. Similarly, if things are more or less true, good, or noble, it must be that they reflect or participate to various degrees in that which is the fullest manifestation of these qualities. In arguing thus, Aquinas assumes, with the Platonists, that the most degree of value is necessarily associated with the most degree of reality. So he concludes that since degrees of value imply an ultimate source of value, there is a supreme being in which all perfections are realized.

The fifth way argues from the evidence of design in the world. Aquinas notes that most of nature is blind and unintelligent, yet it seems to be orderly and to achieve purposeful ends. To use philosophical terminology, Aquinas believes the world is a **teleological** system. However, an end that does not yet exist cannot direct its own realization. Only if the final goal is contained in the mind of an intelligent architect who guides the process can we account for the existence of a well-designed system. So, Aquinas concludes that "some intelligent being exists by whom all natural things are directed to their end."

A few points need to be clarified concerning these arguments. Contrary to what some of his critics assume, Aquinas never uses the principle that "everything must have a cause" in his argument, because this would lead to the absurd question of "What caused God?" This formulation of the causal principle would be as false as saying that "everything that emits light must have received its light from something else," which would mean that the light of the flashlight must get its light from another light source. Instead, Aquinas is actually claiming that "everything which is merely potential (and thus is dependent and not self-sufficient) must be caused by some other actuality." This principle shows why everything in nature requires an ultimate first cause, but it does not include God in its scope.

Another confusion is that some critics assume that Aquinas's arguments are seeking to prove that the world had a beginning in time. These critics suppose that if we can show it is possible that the world always existed, this will undermine the necessity for a first cause of the world. On the contrary, Aristotle both believed that the world was eternal *and* that it required an Unmoved Mover. Although Aquinas does not believe the arguments given for the eternity of the world are conclusive, he does think this is logically possible. Why then would an always existing universe require a first cause? To illustrate the type of answer Aquinas gives, try to imagine an oil lamp with a flame that existed from all eternity. The flame would have existed for an infinite amount of time in the past. Nevertheless, from all eternity, the flame's existence would have depended on the oil that sustains it. If the oil had not existed, neither would the flame. Thus, even though the flame was eternal, it would have been an eternally dependent entity. Similarly, even if the world had been eternal, it still would have needed an ultimate cause to sustain it.

This means that when Aquinas says God is the first cause, he does not mean that God is necessarily a *temporally* first cause. He is not talking about a horizontal causal series stretching through time, but about a vertical causal series, operating right here and now with God at the apex. In other words, Aquinas's picture of God's causal relationship to the world is really not like that of the colliding pool balls, where we are talking about a linear, temporal series of causes and effects. Instead, his vision of the universe is better illustrated by our example of the hanging chain, where the series of dependent causes and effects are contemporary with one another and where, at each moment of their existence, they continuously depend on some self-sufficient cause to support them. For this reason, God is primarily a continuously sustaining cause and not necessarily an initiating cause.

Although Aquinas thinks the eternity of the world is consistent with his theistic arguments, he does not think we can prove the world always existed. Can we then prove the world must have had a beginning in time? Some medieval philosophers such as St. Bonaventure thought that we could logically prove just that. However, Aquinas does not find such arguments persuasive either (ST 1.46.1,2). Hence, this issue is not something reason can resolve. As a matter of fact, Aquinas does believe the world had a beginning, but says the only way we can know this is that the book of Genesis in the Bible tells us so. It is an issue to be resolved by revelation, not by philosophy as Aristotle and Bonaventure thought.

Aquinas claims his five proofs have established the existence of a supreme being who is an unchanging, uncaused, intrinsically necessary being, and who is an absolutely perfect, purposeful cause. At least two general criticisms have been raised against the proofs as a whole. First, why couldn't we conclude that each of the preceding five properties apply to different beings? If there are five different proofs, maybe there are five different gods. His answer is that different beings are distinguished by the fact that they have different properties. All the proofs point to a being who is absolutely perfect and unlimited. If two beings were perfect in every respect, they would have identical properties and would really be the same. Furthermore, there cannot be two unlimited beings, for then they would limit each other and would no longer be unlimited. Hence, there is only one God.

The second criticism concerns the fact that Aquinas ends each argument with different variations on the phrase "And this everyone understands to be God." Both religious and non-religious critics say that the abstract metaphysical cause talked of by these arguments is a far cry from the personal, loving God of the Bible. Aquinas does not claim the proofs give us a complete picture of God. This is why he believes revelation must supplement reason. But he would insist that they do give us some of the more important qualities of God. For example, the fourth proof shows that God is ultimate perfection. Since, by his definition, a perfect being must be perfect in goodness and love, this suggests that the ultimate being is a personal being.

Because of these five arguments, Thomas Aquinas has an established place in history as one of the most forceful proponents of natural theology. However, not everyone was convinced that he had successfully provided a rational proof of God's existence. When we get to David Hume and Immanuel Kant in the eighteenth century, these arguments come under some fresh criticism.

THE PROBLEM OF RELIGIOUS LANGUAGE

A problem that lurks in all discussions of God is the problem of religious language. How can we speak about an infinite and perfect being if the language we speak is drawn from the world of finite and imperfect creatures? For example, we may use the word *good* to talk about a friend. However, if we then say, "God is good," it seems we are saying God is good in the same sense our friend is good. But surely this will not do, for God's goodness cannot be equated with human goodness. Therefore, the positive terms we use to talk about humans cannot be used univocally (with the same meaning) to talk about God. Must we then use a word such as *good* equivocally (with different meanings) when we talk about humans and about God? For example, when we say that a trumpet's pitch, a bottle of soda, and a pancake are all "flat," the word has a completely different meaning in each case. However, this explanation doesn't work either. First, if all our knowledge begins with experience, as Aquinas believes, then the meaning of our terms, even those that apply to God, must have some origin in the realm of human experience. We cannot use terms that apply to God uniquely, since we lack the direct experience of God's essence that would be necessary to give these terms their special meaning. Second, Aquinas *does* want to say there is *some* similarity between human and divine goodness, even if they are not exactly the same, for humans are created in the image of God.

Aquinas's first solution is the negative way. This approach was common among the earlier medieval thinkers and is the favorite solution of the mystics. The negative way claims we can speak of God's properties by negating the proper-

ties common to finite creatures. For example, we may say God is immutable (without change), eternal (not bound by time), or incorporeal (lacking a physical body). However, it is never sufficient to define something in terms of what that thing is *not*. We must be capable of asserting something positive about God.

The second approach, therefore, is the way of analogy. This method lets us start from an object *A* that is directly known and then to go on to infer information about an object *B* that is not directly known. For example, I do not know what it is like to have the responsibilities of the nation's President. However, I have been a president of a local organization and do know what it is like to have minor responsibilities. Since I know that the position of U.S. President is of overwhelming importance compared to that of the president of a small organization, I can know by analogy that the responsibilities of national leadership are proportionally greater than the responsibilities of local leadership. Hence, if we know what it is like for a friend to be good, wise, and intelligent within the limitations of human nature, and if such human properties are diminished approximations of God's attributes, then we can have some knowledge of what goodness, wisdom, and intelligence would mean when attributed to an infinite being.

Moral Philosophy: Human Nature and Divine Law

TELEOLOGICAL ETHICS

As one would expect, Thomas Aquinas's moral theory is a Christian adaptation of Aristotle's *Nicomachean Ethics*. Following in Aristotle's footsteps, Aquinas's ethics is rooted in his teleological metaphysics. Every event in the universe, he says, whether it is the falling of a stone or the blossoming of a fruit tree, occurs because there is some end toward which it is directed. As with the rest of nature, humans have their own natural ends and inclinations. However, we are the only earthly creatures that can consciously choose if and how we will fulfill a given end. Ethics, then, concerns what ends are worthy for humans to pursue. Hence, the moral good is not something alien to us, but is the fulfillment of our natural end. Conversely, evil is a kind of deficiency or privation. It prevents us from achieving fulfillment.

Aquinas says that all genuine actions are either good or bad, none are morally indifferent (ST 1-2.18.9). This is because deliberately chosen actions always seek to achieve some end that will be good or bad. Aquinas makes a distinction between human actions and the acts of humans (ST 1-2.1.1). The former are voluntary, consciously willed actions chosen because the person's reason seeks some end. The latter are simply unconscious or involuntary behaviors, such as absentmindedly scratching one's head or a sneeze. These latter behaviors are neither morally good nor bad. Only voluntary, deliberative actions have moral qualities. Aquinas definitely makes the intellect primary in ethics. Although the will naturally desires what is good, it needs reason to tell it what genuinely is good and the appropriate means for achieving the good.

Aquinas gives three factors that determine whether or not an action is morally good or evil. These are (1) the *object* of the action, (2) the *circumstances*, and (3) the *end* that is sought. To use Aquinas's example, giving alms to the poor is an action that has as its object the transfer of money to a needy person. Taken in isolation, this object is good. However, the circumstances play some role in the moral evaluation of the action. If the money I gave was stolen, then the goodness of the object is tarnished by the evil of the circumstances. Or if the person's needs are trivial, but the financial burdens of my family are urgent, the circumstances would again affect the moral quality of the action. Finally, even if the object and the circumstances were morally good, if the end I was trying to achieve was merely public praise, then the end or motive would not be morally worthy. Since these three factors may differ in their goodness or badness, Aquinas says that an action is not *absolutely* good unless the object, circumstances, and end are all good.

Thus far, Aquinas's moral theory is fairly consistent with the Aristotelian model. However, there is a problem. Aristotle has a purely naturalistic ethics. He treats humans as though they were simply one species among many in nature. Although Aristotle believes humans are unique in that they are rational, he has no sense that we have a spiritual nature and a special relationship to God. For example, his ethics contains no notion of obedience to divine commands. For humans as natural creatures, the final end of our life is the happiness and self-fulfillment found in the appropriate development of all categories of human excellence, particularly that of intellectual virtue. Aquinas believed that Aristotle gave us a vision of the imperfect and temporal happiness humans can achieve in this life through our natural resources. It is as good an ethics as we will ever find, *as far as it goes*. However, for Aquinas's Christian understanding of human life, the naturalistic ethics of Aristotle did not go far enough. We yearn for the good in its fullest form. But any good found in the natural realm can only be a particular and imperfect, finite good. Nature does not provide the means to fulfill our spiritual nature, but points beyond itself to what does fulfill us. If the purpose of our life is possession of the supreme good, this can only be found in God himself. This is not found in mere knowledge about God, but through acquaintance with God, achieved in the vision of the divine essence. Since knowledge of God attainable in this life is always imperfect, our natural desire for ultimate fulfillment points to the necessity of an afterlife.

THE NATURAL LAW

Because we were created by God to live a certain way, we can reflect on human nature and discover certain natural guidelines that will help us actualize our human potentialities. This is what Aquinas calls the **natural law** in morality.* Since human nature stays basically the same from culture to culture and century to century, the precepts of the

---

*The notion of the natural law in morality was introduced by the Greeks and developed by the Stoics. It was also a central feature of Augustine's early moral philosophy in *On Free Choice of the Will.*

natural law are universal and self-evident to reason. Previously, we had said that an action is absolutely good if the object, circumstances, and end are good. But how do we determine when these are good? The answer is that the good is what is in accordance with reason, and this is defined as being in conformity to the natural law of morality. Following his hierarchy from the lowest forms of life on through the higher animals and up to human life, Aquinas seeks to show that by reflecting on what is in accord with nature and our natural inclinations, we can derive moral principles. First of all, there is a natural tendency among all creatures to preserve their own life. The principle "Life is to be preserved" comes from this. Specifically, for Aquinas this means that not only murder but also suicide would violate natural law. Second, all animals seek to preserve their species and care for their offspring. For humans, this requires not only obvious biological and emotional nurturing of our young, but also educating our children and helping them achieve all their potential. Third, since we are higher than the beasts, we have an inclination to fully realize all our rational, human capacities. This leads to the obligation to pursue truth (including the knowledge of God) and to follow all the precepts necessary to live harmoniously in society.

If the natural law is universal and available to every rational creature, why don't all people agree on it? The answer is that they are blinded by passion, bad habits, and ignorance (ST 1-2.94.6). Thus, the person who is unaware of the natural law is like a color-blind person. In both cases, the person has limited capacities and cannot perceive reality normally. Some people think that something like the natural moral law is programed within our conscience. However, for Aquinas, the conscience is not a source of knowledge as much as it is the rational activity of applying moral knowledge to particular cases (ST 1.79.13). But what if reason errs in making such moral judgments? For example, suppose our reason tells us that something evil is good or that what is really good is forbidden? Ignorance can cause us to have a clear conscience while doing wrong and a guilty conscience for

doing something that is right. Aquinas answers that "every will at variance with reason, whether right or erring, is always evil" (ST 1-2.19.5). In other words, the most that can be asked of people is that they follow their informed conscience to the best of their ability. If our conscience is objectively mistaken, we are still judged by how we followed the moral light as we perceived it.

THE FOUR LAWS

For Aquinas it is important to show the link between morality and metaphysics. Hence, he explains that the moral law written into our nature is an expression of God's eternal law. Contrary to the voluntarists, Aquinas believes that the moral law is not based on the arbitrary decision of God's will but is an expression of the divine reason, which is rooted in God's nature. Since God's nature is not arbitrary, neither is the moral law.

Aquinas believes that there are actually four kinds of laws or, more accurately, four ways in which God's law is manifested. In each case, the law is rooted in the rational order that God created. First of all, there is the *eternal law*, the rational order that the ruler of the universe established for his creation. All things are subject to the eternal law. The apples falling to the earth and flames rising to the sky all manifest the order created by the eternal law. Thus, for Aquinas, the phrase "the laws of nature" is more than a metaphor. Although all of nature follows the eternal law blindly, only humans can reflect on the moral dimensions of God's law and we alone have the capacity to obey it or disobey it. Second, the *natural law* (which has already been discussed) is the law available to reason that governs human moral behavior. The natural law guides us insofar as we are natural and social creatures. It leads us to fulfill the Aristotelian model of moral character by developing the classical Greek virtues of temperance, courage, justice, and wisdom. Third, there is the *divine law*, which is given to us in revelation. The divine law goes beyond natural law and guides us in achieving eternal happiness. In following this law, the natural virtues are surpassed by the theological virtues of faith, hope, and love. Unlike the natural virtues, however, these can only be attained through the workings of God's grace (ST 1-2.62.1). The fourth kind of law is the *human law* instituted by governments. However, if such law is legitimate, it too is rooted in God's eternal law. Hence in obeying a legitimate law, we are obeying God. Quoting Augustine, Aquinas says, "in temporal law there is nothing just and lawful but what man has drawn from the eternal law" (ST 1-2.93.3). In his discussion of the human or temporal law, Aquinas's political philosophy emerges.

Political Philosophy

In the eight hundred years from Augustine to Aquinas one finds few significant discussions of the nature of the political state in medieval philosophy. The dominance of Neoplatonism in this period led philosophers to be concerned mainly with eternal realities and the questions of metaphysics and logic. However, as Aristotle's complete works became available, philosophers once again began to address questions of political theory. Also, as society became more stable and civilization flourished, philosophical questions concerning the nature of the state, the law, and political obligation became more of a concern.

Aquinas's political philosophy focuses on the nature of political laws. He defines law as "an ordinance of reason for the common good, promulgated by him who has care of the community" (ST 1-2.90.4). Some laws are concerned with elaborating and enforcing the natural law (such as laws against murder and theft). These sorts of laws should be the same everywhere. However, other laws set out details left open by the natural law and are instituted for the sake of uniformity in a particular society. For example, laws stating what penalties should be imposed for particular crimes are not detailed in the natural law. In our own day, the law in the United States dictates that cars should drive on the right side of the road, whereas other countries may specify the left side of the road. Although the details are arbitrary, such laws ensure human safety and follow from the universal prin-

ciple that life should be preserved. However, whether directly or indirectly, all civil laws receive their validity from the principles of the natural law. Any human law that violates natural law is not a genuine law at all and does not require our obedience. In some cases, it is the lesser evil to obey laws, to keep the peace, while in other cases civil disobedience in the name of the higher law may be necessary (ST 1-2.96.4).

What should be the extent of law? Thomas says that a human attempt to illegalize all forms of immoral behavior would be self-defeating, because human nature would make such a goal impossible to realize. If every form of wrong behavior were illegal, we would all be in jail! Generally, law should be concerned only with major evils, namely, those that harm others and undermine an ordered human society. In other words, human law is restricted to the sphere of people in their mutual relations (ST 1-2.100.2). Hence, political legislation is to concern itself only with justice, and should refrain from issues that concern the spiritual community and private, individual morality.

According to Aquinas, civil society is natural and requires no justification. His position agrees with that of the Greeks. However, it contrasts with that of Augustine, who thought government was a necessary evil brought into being in response to human perversity. It also disagrees with the Enlightenment philosophers, who tended to see society as an artificially created order. For this reason, they felt the need to develop theories explaining why government was justified. But Aquinas says that even "in the state of innocence [humans] would have led a social life" (ST 1.96.4). He goes on to argue that any society always requires some system of governance and someone to look after the common good, so human nature necessitates the institution of government. Although government as such does not need to be justified, he does say that any particular form of government or the authority of any particular leader does need some warrant. For Aquinas, the ideal state combines different elements. It has one ruler, whose power is balanced by other governing bodies, all of whom are selected by the will of the people (ST 1-2.105.1).

Evaluation and Significance

THE REJECTION OF PLATONIC DUALISM

Aquinas presents nature as a unified and continuous spectrum of beings from the rocks and plants, up to the lowliest larvae, and then to the higher animals, until we reach the apex with those creatures capable of reason, free choice, moral decisions, and spiritual life, namely, humans and angels. This picture was influenced by the Neoplatonists and Augustine, yet Aquinas rejects the Platonic assumption that the physical world is a shadow world that is not fully real. This dualistic theme in Plato unfortunately suggested a tension between the spiritual realm and the natural, physical world. For Aquinas, however, physical nature is not alien to the spiritual dimension, for this entire "chain of being" pointed to and found its final end in God. This metaphysical vision enabled Aquinas to give more weight to the biblical doctrine of the goodness of creation. In contrast to Platonic Christianity, Aquinas did not view the body as an unfortunate prison in which the soul resides. Instead, the body is important for knowledge, and it is what makes us the unique individuals we are. In this way, he enabled his contemporaries to rediscover their humanity. Not only are we spiritual beings with an eternal destiny, but we are a part of nature as well. By giving more importance to the physical world and our here-and-now, earthly existence, Thomas Aquinas provided a better foundation for the works of human culture such as science, politics, law, and the arts than was possible in an Augustinian picture of the world.

SCIENCE AND THEOLOGY

Aquinas's focus on the physical world and the value of natural explanations raised the question of the relationship between science and theology. This would prove an important question that would be continuously debated all the way into our century. It is useful, therefore, to examine the insights and problems of Aquinas's position on this issue. The problem he faced was that on the one hand, science explains events in terms of physical causes. On the other hand, he viewed nature as governed by divine providence. His teleological argument for God, found in the fifth way, emphasizes that events in nature can only be explained if we see them as fulfilling God's purposes. We have, then, two kinds of explanations. Is the life-giving rain caused by the moisture-saturated clouds, or is it provided by God's benevolence? Is a newborn baby a result of biological causes, or is it a gift from God? To answer these questions, Aquinas develops a theory of dual causality, drawing on Aristotle's theory that different sorts of causes explain a particular event:

> It is . . . clear that the same effect is ascribed to a natural cause and to God, not as though part were effected by God and part by the natural agent; but the whole effect proceeds from each, yet in different ways, just as the whole of one and the same effect is ascribed to the instrument, again the whole is ascribed to the principal agent.[2]

To illustrate Aquinas's point, when someone comes into my kitchen and asks, "Why is the water boiling?" two completely different answers could be given, both equally correct. I could give a *scientific* answer in terms of the immediate *efficient and material causes* and say, "The water is boiling *because* the fire is heating the bottom of the pot, which is transferring its heat to the water, which is causing air bubbles to rise to the surface." On the other hand, I could provide a *teleological* answer in terms of the *final cause* and simply say, "The water is boiling *because* I am going to cook some potatoes." The two answers appeal to different principles and serve different purposes, but they are completely complementary. In the same way, Aquinas believes we can explain natural events in terms of natural causes, without having to abandon our belief in God's providence and governance of the world. Although the physical properties, laws, and materials of creation are what immediately cause natural events to occur, it is God who has orchestrated this order of nature to carry out his will. Thus, Aquinas might say it is appropriate to think about both the physical properties of clouds *and* God's benevolence when trying to explain the fact that the rain falls and nourishes our crops. This way of reconciling the scientific and religious views of the world would be important to many of the thinkers in the modern period who were both scientists and Christians.

It is significant that Aquinas was seeking a way to reconcile the science of his day with a theistic vision of the universe. In doing so, he certainly provided a richer basis for pursuing a scientific knowledge of the world than the otherworldly approach of some medievals. Nevertheless, as we shall see when we get to the Renaissance, a major shortcoming of Aquinas's project lies—in the phrase just used—in "the science of his day." Because the science available to people at this time was Aristotelian science, not only did their theological explanations of natural events use teleology, but their scientific explanations were infected with it too. They thought every part of nature was trying to fulfill its divinely appointed end. The stone falls because its natural end is to be reunited with the earth. The acorn grows into an oak tree because this is its natural purpose. As you can see, explaining natural events in terms of the purposes they are meant to fulfill provides only a rather thin and inadequate explanation of things. The Aristotelian emphasis on essences meant that nature was mainly understood in terms of eternal and logical relationships rather than temporal and causal ones. Thus, even though Aquinas gave more importance to physical processes than Christian theologians ever had before, only when people abandoned the Aristotelian model of providing teleological explanations of events could science mature. Instead of speculating how the purposes and ends of natural things fit into God's plan, scientists eventually learned to pay more attention to the details and regularities of the material and efficient causes themselves.

With Aquinas, we reach the culmination of medieval philosophy. In the following chapter, we survey the intellectual causes that played a role in unraveling the fabric of Scholasticism.

Questions for Understanding

1. How did Aquinas attempt to reconcile the spheres of faith and reason?

2. What is the meaning of "natural theology"? How does Aquinas illustrate this concept?

3. According to Aquinas, how do reason and experience both contribute to knowledge? Why do we need both?

4. Using Aquinas's Aristotelian metaphysics, explain what happens when the wood in a tree is transformed into a bookcase.

5. What does Aquinas mean by "essence"? How is the relationship between essence and existence different for God than it is for any other creature?

6. Why does Aquinas reject Anselm's ontological argument?

7. Briefly describe the five kinds of arguments Aquinas uses to prove God's existence.

8. State in your own words what it means to say that Aquinas believes the world is a "teleological system"?

9. Since Aquinas believed that the world needs a cause, why does he also believe that it is logically possible that the world had always existed? What does he mean by "cause" here?

10. What is the problem of religious language? What are several ways that Aquinas attempts to solve it?

11. In Aquinas's ethics, what three factors determine the rightness or wrongness of an action?

12. What does the term "natural law" mean in the context of ethics? How does Aquinas use this notion in developing his ethical theory?

13. Why does Aquinas believe that there are four different kinds of laws? What is their relationship?

14. According to Aquinas, what is the basis of our civil laws? What sorts of activities should be regulated by law?

15. How does Aquinas attempt to harmonize scientific explanations with theological explanations of the world?

Questions for Reflection

1. In what ways is Aquinas's philosophy more like Aristotle's than Plato's? What were some of the consequences of Aquinas's rejection of Platonic dualism?

2. Basing your answer on Aquinas's philosophy, give an example of something that can only be known by reason but not by faith. What is something that can only be known by faith? What is an example of a truth that can be known both by faith (revelation) and reason?

3. Imagine that you are Aquinas. A very pious critic (such as Tertullian in chapter 7) says that Christian philosophers should not be borrowing from non-Christian thought such as Aristotle's philosophy. How would Aquinas reply to this objection?

4. Which one of Aquinas's arguments for God do you think is the strongest? Why? Which one do you think is the weakest? Why?

5. Using Aquinas's three criteria for determining the moral worth of an action, evaluate the morality of each of the following actions: (a) sticking a knife in a person to cause him pain, (b) a surgeon sticking a knife into a patient on the operating table to remove a tumor, (c) saving the life of a person by giving her medicine, (d) accidentally saving the life of a person by giving her medicine when you mistakenly thought it was poison, (e) stealing money to give to a charity, (f) giving your own money to a charity because of the good publicity it will bring to your political campaign.

6. Think of examples from human behavior that would support Aquinas's notion that there is a universal moral law. Think of some examples that would count against this view.

7. For the purposes of this exercise, assume that you agree with Aquinas's view of natural law and political philosophy. In the light of his philosophy, develop arguments to show that the law should either permit or forbid each of the following activities: (a) slavery, (b) pornography, (c) abortion, (d) (an issue of your choice).

8. Suppose someone says that modern science has eliminated the need for God in explaining the world. How might Aquinas respond?

Notes

1. This and other references to *Summa Theologica* are symbolized as ST. Quotations are taken from *Basic Writings of Saint Thomas Aquinas*, 2 vols., ed. Anton C. Pegis (New York: Random House, 1945). The three numbers in the references refer to the numbers of the part, question, and article.

2. *Summa Contra Gentiles* 3.70, in *Basic Writings of Saint Thomas Aquinas*, vol. 2.

12

The Unraveling of the Medieval Synthesis

IN THE PERIOD FROM 1300 TO 1500, THE MIGHTY stream of medieval thought developed a rapid succession of shifting currents, breaking it into a number of separate rivulets, each seeking its own, new direction. The philosophical changes are what concern us here; these did not occur in isolation from the social, economic, and political changes that affected every area of European life at this time. By the thirteenth century, the spiritual prestige and political power of the papacy had declined. Many in the fold were scandalized by the series of worldly popes and cardinals that tarnished the ideals of the Church. The excessive wealth and privilege of the Church produced calls for reform among some and a retreat from the institutional Church into personal piety among others. The criticisms of the Church by John Wyclif in England and John Huss in Bohemia provided early forewarnings of the Reformation. Furthermore, the confusion of spiritual authority with political allegiances produced the Great Schism from 1378 to 1415, when there were two rival popes, a French pope in Avignon and an Italian pope in Rome.

The Church had to deal not only with a crisis of authority and spiritual disillusionment, but with shifting political currents as well. For centuries, the Church had been a powerful international organization that prospered in the context of weak secular states. However, the dissension within the Church played into the hands of the rising powers among the political states. As Europe grew richer, the secular kingdoms became more autonomous from Rome. The rediscovery of Aristotle's *Politics* promoted the viewpoint that the state was a natural entity, which was justified on moral and rational grounds, rather than an institution that received its authority from God and the Church. However, the secular kingdoms did not lack turmoil. The Hundred Years War between England and France fueled the spirit of nationalism. Furthermore, the times were characterized by economic and social unrest, and peasants' revolts broke out in France and England. Despite these problems, however, by the last half of the fifteenth century the emerging emphasis on royal sovereignty culminated in strong monarchies in England, France, and Spain, which would be major players in western European life for centuries to come. These states did not sever their relationship with the Church, but their reliance on it severely diminished. These and other factors threatened the rigid stability of the medieval scheme of things. The taken-for-granted triad of hierarchy, authority, and unity were ideals that had dominated people's spiritual, intellectual, and political lives for centuries. However, these three pillars of the Middle Ages were now beginning to crumble.

While these controversies and changes were occurring in the larger society, a number of the influential philosophers of the fourteenth century began to move away from some of the essential principles of Scholasticism. This marked the beginning of the decline of medieval philosophy. Although they chipped away at the intellectual foundations of the Scholastic systems, these thinkers did so from the standpoint of a sincere Christian faith. They were convinced that faith was best served by freeing it from entanglements with philosophy. The driving force of their thought was a strong emphasis on the omnipotence of God. Their religious creed dictated that God's actions are totally free and beyond the ability of reason to analyze or explain.

To preview this chapter, the focus on the absolute power of God led to a number of radical conclusions. The first was *antirationalism*. Aquinas believed an all-powerful God can do whatever is logically possible. However, the critics who followed claimed that the realm of the possible is larger than Aquinas ever imagined. Hence, reason is not competent to determine the way the world is or must be. The desire to limit reason took the form of empiricism in some thinkers and of mysticism in others. The second feature of this period was *nominalism*. Universals were held in suspicion,

and the concrete reality of individuals was upheld. Third, *confidence in natural theology declined*. Philosophers argued that doctrines such as the existence of God and the immortality of the human soul could not be definitively proven by reason, as Aquinas had thought. They claimed these doctrines can only be known and affirmed on the basis of revelation and faith. Fourth, *voluntarism* became the central theme in ethics. This position claims that the will has priority over the intellect. If God's intellect does not impose limits on his will, then he is completely free in choosing what is morally good. This means that human reason cannot determine what is morally good. Thus, moral obligation is not a matter of following reason's directions but in obeying God's sovereign commands. Fifth, the ideas of this century provided *a new approach to natural science*. If no rational forms guided God's free creation of the world, then the world is completely contingent. Human reason employed in metaphysical speculation cannot tell us what the world is like. Only observation will tell us what sort of world God made. As Etienne Gilson described this stage of philosophy,

> *After a brief honeymoon [one might almost have said, before the wedding breakfast was over], theology and philosophy think they see that their marriage was a mistake. While waiting for the decree of divorce, which is not long in coming, they proceed to divide their effects. Each resumes possession of its own problems, and warns the other against interference.*[1]

The grounds for this divorce were laid by such thinkers as John Duns Scotus, William of Ockham, and the mystic Meister Eckhart.

JOHN DUNS SCOTUS

The Subtle Scottish Professor

Little is known for sure about John Duns Scotus's life. He was born somewhere around 1266 in Scotland.* As a young man, he entered the Franciscan order and went on to study at Oxford and Paris, exhibiting a sharp mind and an aptitude for mathematics. He spent his life lecturing and writing at Oxford, Paris, and Cologne. After working in the latter city for only a year, he died in 1308, in his early forties. The authenticity of Scotus's works is very much disputed. Some works are clearly authentic, while others once attributed to him are now known to be unauthentic, and scholars disagree about yet other manuscripts. Duns Scotus is difficult to read, because he is not a clear writer. Nevertheless, most agree that the difficulty of his writings stems as much from his intellectually challenging and subtle arguments as from his lack of writing skills. In fact, his contemporaries called him Doctor Subtilis ("The Subtle Doctor"). He had many followers, who were known as "Dunsmen" or "dunces." They were the prime objects of vilification by the Renaissance humanists, who viewed them and their Scholastic philosophy as barriers to enlightenment and intellectual progress. As a result, the name *dunce* came to mean a dull, ignorant person.

Theory of Knowledge: Restricting Reason

In this brief summary, we will ignore the overly complicated details of Scotus's epistemology and simply note his differences with Thomas Aquinas on the issue of faith and reason. Scotus agrees with Aquinas that there can be no conflict between truths of faith and truths of reason, and he uses philosophical reasoning to defend his theories. But Duns Scotus restricts the sphere of reason much more than Aquinas did. Scotus's studies in mathematics gave him a model of what real demonstration was, and by comparison a great deal of Aquinas's arguments in natural theology fell short. Although he agreed with Aquinas that the Trinity cannot be proven by reason, Scotus also excluded from rational discussion or proof such topics as a number of the aspects of God's nature, as well as divine providence and the immortality of soul. Only faith can give us certainty in these matters, he claimed. Contrary to the Thomistic position,† philosophy and theology are completely different types of inquiry for Scotus. Whereas philosophy is a theoretical discipline, the knowledge sought for in theology, he says, "should be described as practical."[2] Scotus's attempt to impose limits on the sphere of reason was the first step in the unraveling of the Scholastic synthesis of faith and reason. Later thinkers would be much more radical in limiting reason.

Metaphysics: Moving Away from Scholasticism

UNIVERSALS AND INDIVIDUALITY

On the issue of universals, Scotus avoids all the traditional answers. Contrary to the realists, he claims that only individuals are real, but in opposition to the nominalists he believed that universals do have some objective reality. Although this would seem to place him in agreement with Aquinas, they differ on what distinguishes one individual of a species from another. Aquinas thought that it had to be their individual matter that distinguished Socrates from Plato, because they both exemplify the same form of humanity. However, Scotus argues that

*"Scotus" means "the Scot." In Scotus's time, unlike that of John Scotus Erigena four centuries earlier, only inhabitants of Scotland, and not the Irish, were called Scots.

†The adjective *Thomistic* is derived from the name "Thomas of Aquinas."

since matter is an indefinite bundle of potentialities, it cannot define the concrete individuality of a Socrates. Nor can something so indefinite be the object of knowledge. If the Thomistic answer fails, how does Scotus think we can have knowledge of individuals? Since Scotus retained the Aristotelian assumption that we can only know forms, if we can know concrete individuals at all, a form must constitute each individual thing. Inherent in the universal nature (the essence or *whatness* of any particular) is the individual nature (its *thisness*). The Latin term for this individuating difference is *haecceitas*. Just as there is a form of humanity, so there is a form unique to Socrates and one unique to Plato that are the unique but fully knowable features of each person. The form of "human" does not exist separately from "Platoneity" (as we may call Plato's unique form), but it may be distinguished in a formal way. Although this attempt to combine a Greek notion of universals with a greater focus on individuality is somewhat complicated, Duns Scotus's emphasis on the reality of individuals took a beginning step away from the worldview of the medieval thinkers.

NATURAL THEOLOGY

Concerning arguments for the existence of God, Scotus seems to agree with Aquinas that such demonstrations must be based on our experience of the world. However, he questions the absolute certainty of most of the Thomistic proofs. For example, he says the argument from motion shows there must be a first mover. However, any proof taken from the physical world cannot go beyond the physical world. Hence, this argument limits us to the world of motion and does not give us a necessary divine being that is the cause of all other beings. However, Scotus does find some value in reconstructed versions of the arguments from efficient causality and contingency. Finally, unlike Thomas, he does find value in Anselm's ontological argument but thinks it needs to be "touched up" with a premise stating that a necessary being is possible. However, he thinks the only evidence we can give for the possibility of such a being is some "persuasive considerations." In doing so, he

changes it into an empirical and probabilistic argument. In summary, Duns Scotus believed the theistic arguments were considerably weaker than Aquinas supposed, for they tend to be probability arguments only and not rigorous demonstrations.

Duns Scotus similarly differs with Aquinas on the issue of immortality. Thomas Aquinas believed the human soul necessarily survived the death of the body. Once again, Scotus says this is a matter of probability only. After all, God could have created the soul in such a way that it would perish with the body. Although it is reasonable to suppose the soul is immortal, this cannot be demonstrated. Our certainty that the soul was, in fact, given an immortal nature by God is based on faith alone. This is a good example of the way in which these late medieval writers tended to give faith sovereignty over much of the domain that Thomas Aquinas thought should be shared with reason.

Moral Philosophy and the Primacy of the Will

An important issue in both the psychology and the ethics of medieval philosophy was the relationship between the will and the intellect.* For Aquinas, the intellect was the higher, nobler, and more worthy faculty of the soul. For Duns Scotus, however, the will is superior to the intellect, a claim that aligns him with voluntarism and Augustine's later thought. Scotus's arguments are that, first, knowledge is simply an instrument of the will. The intellect provides the will with information and alternatives, but it is the will that decides between the alternatives. Second, the will can move the intellect in the sense that we can choose what we will think about. Third, the will is completely free and cannot be determined by anything, including the intellect. Thomas Aquinas agreed with the Greeks that we necessarily will what we think to be the highest good. However, Scotus asserts that the will is not determined by a knowledge of the good, but only chooses the good

---

*See Chapter 10 for the initial discussion of this issue.

if it freely decides to do so. Whereas the intellect is determined by the object known, the will can accept or reject what is brought before it. Hence, "the total cause of willing in the will is the will."[3] Whereas Aquinas's intellectualism dictated that we find eternal blessedness in contemplating God, Scotus's voluntarism led him to say that we find blessedness in the love of God, an act of the will that unites us with him. Hence, Scotus does not agree with Aquinas that morality is based on the natural tendency to pursue happiness. Instead, morality may require an act of justice that interferes with our own advantage and happiness. The obligations of morality depend solely on what God commands, independent of considerations of personal happiness. Aquinas thought we can discern the moral law by studying human nature, but Duns Scotus thought there is no way to learn ethical truths by natural means.

This voluntarism also applies to God. His actions are not determined by his reason. Duns Scotus thought this must be the case if God is completely free and fully omnipotent. Consequently, our reason cannot know his purposes or deduce his actions from *a priori* principles. Since all things are contingent on the free will of God, there is no rational necessity to things and the universe could have been otherwise than it is. If God's choices were logically necessary, we could reason out the details of the world like a system of Euclidean geometry. Since we cannot do so, it is clear God was free in creating the world and, hence, the features of creation are all contingent.

The command to love God is the only moral law concerned with what is good in itself. All other actions are good simply because they are commanded by God and not because of the ends they achieve. However, Scotus qualifies this point by saying that the first set of commands in the Ten Commandments are rationally necessary moral truths. These are the commands that say you should have no other gods but the one true God, you should not make any idols, you should not take the name of the Lord your God in vain, and you should remember the Sabbath day to keep it holy. Scotus argues that these commands follow from God's love of himself, and it would be self-contradictory for him to command otherwise. Hence, if there is any natural law, it is to be found here. However, the rest of the divine commandments are products of God's sovereign will, and therefore they are not rationally necessary. Their only claim on our conscience is that God commanded them. Presumably, God could have just as easily decreed that murder, adultery, and stealing were not wrong.

In summary, although John Duns Scotus differed from the thinkers of the thirteenth century on a number of points, in many ways he was continuous with them. He serves as a transitional figure to the later theologians (such as William of Ockham) who took what were mere tendencies in Scotus and carried them to their furthest extreme.

WILLIAM OF OCKHAM

Ockham's Controversial Life

William of Ockham was born sometime between 1280 and 1290 in the village of Ockham, near London. He entered the Franciscan order at an early age and studied theology at Oxford. Although he had completed his courses and had begun lecturing and writing, he never achieved his master's degree because some suspected that he had embraced dangerous and heretical doctrines. The end result was that in 1324 he was summoned to the papal court in Avignon, France, and was forced to remain there for four years while a commission of theologians investigated the charges of heresy. He filled these years of waiting by writing on theology, philosophy, and physics. In 1327, while still at Avignon, he became involved in a controversy over how literally St. Francis's vow of poverty should be interpreted. Ockham sided with the head of the Franciscan order in condemning the materialism and excesses of the papacy and in attempting to return the Church back to Francis's ideal of a simple lifestyle. In 1328 it became clear that Pope John XXII was about to issue an official condemnation of their position. Consequently, Ockham and his superior fled and sought the protection of Emperor Louis of Bavaria. On his arrival, Ockham supposedly said to the Emperor, "Protect me with your sword, and I will defend you with my pen." Ockham and the others involved in the revolt were excommunicated by the Pope. Ockham then took up residence in Munich and continued to write. At this point in his life, he moved into more extreme political positions and wrote tracts opposing the Pope's claim to temporal power. His writings developed a political theory that pointed in the direction of the secularization of politics. After Louis's death in 1347, it appears that Ockham may have sought to be reconciled with Pope Clement VI, but it is not clear whether or not this took place. While the facts of his death are not certain, Ockham is believed to have died in 1349 of the Black Plague that devastated northern Europe at this time.

Ockham's Two Tasks

Ockham's philosophy was guided by two fundamental themes. The first was a very rigorous conception of God's omnipotence. He takes this to be the supreme principle that must inform all our thinking about the world. As he expresses it, "I believe in God, father almighty; which I understand thus, that everything which does not involve a manifest contradiction is to be attributed to the divine power."[4] On the face of it, this sounds like a very pious affirmation of faith. Indeed, for Ockham, it was just that. However, as we will see, from this central conviction he draws some very radical conclusions in the areas of epistemology, metaphysics, and ethics. Basically, he argues that if God is all-powerful, then his creation of the world was not guided by any rational necessities. Everything

in the world is **contingent**.* Since this is the case, then only experience can tell us about the existence of things in the world and their properties.

Ockham's second guiding theme was a rigorous empiricism that condemned any tendencies to go beyond experience by appealing to unnecessary hypothetical or speculative explanations. This was a methodological principle that later writers called **"Ockham's razor"** and that modern scientists now call the "principle of parsimony" or the "principle of economy." One of the ways Ockham expressed it was to say, "What can be explained on fewer principles is explained needlessly by more."[5] This principle works like a razor because it "shaves" off all unnecessary entities in our explanations. Ockham particularly used this principle in his attempts to show that reality can be explained without appeal to the realm of universals. Although this principle was not original to him (it can be found in Aristotle), it followed from Ockham's very austere view of what was really necessary to account for the world. This principle turned out to be very influential in the replacement of Aristotelian science by the much more economical theories of modern science.

Theory of Knowledge: Denying Universals

KNOWLEDGE BEGINS IN EXPERIENCE

Ockham began his epistemology with a strong statement of empiricism. He says all knowledge about the world is grounded in *intuitive knowledge.*† As he expresses it, "Nothing can be naturally known in itself, unless it is known intuitively."[6] Intuitive knowledge includes our perception of external things as well as our immediate awareness of our own inner states such as acts of will, joy, and

---

*The existence of something is contingent if there is no logical contradiction in either supposing that it exists or does not exist. For example, kangaroos exist in our world, but we can imagine a world without them. Hence, kangaroos are contingent beings.
†"Intuition" here does not mean some sort of inner feeling or insight, but refers to whatever is directly evident to the mind.

sorrow. He sometimes refers to intuitive knowledge as "experimental knowledge." Since, under normal conditions, intuitive knowledge is directly related to its object, it can tell us about what does or does not exist.

Any knowledge not related to an object of immediate experience is a derivative form of knowledge called *abstractive knowledge*. This knowledge is a pale residue left in the mind by our original experiences. The objects of these experiences are retained in the mind as concepts or mental signs. Concepts cannot provide evidence of what exists, as does intuitive knowledge, since the object that once produced them may no longer exist. However, they do serve as the vehicles of the understanding. Abstractive knowledge includes the image or memory of a specific thing minus the concrete details of its existence. Abstractive knowledge also includes what we usually call "abstract ideas" or ideas that refer to an entire category of individuals such as "animal," "tree," and "book." These ideas appear to be universals, because they are vague and indistinct representations that gloss over the details of the many particular individuals that were the cause of these ideas. However, they are not true universals, because they lack any sort of metaphysical status of their own.

Ockham's Nominalism

The most important parts of Ockham's epistemology revolve around his theory of signs. A sign is something that stands for or represents something else. There are two kinds of signs: natural and conventional. Natural signs occur whenever an object signifies its cause. For example, smoke is a sign of fire. However, another kind of natural sign is produced by perception when a particular object creates an image or mental picture within us. For example, when we see a red rose it causes a red rose image to be retained in our mind. This kind of sign has some degree of universality because the image will be the same for all people with similar experiences. The mental image or concept is a natural sign of its cause and is able to signify the rose. Conventional signs, in contrast,

are produced when each culture invents words to refer to these mental images.

Some terms are signs of specific individuals, such as "Plato." Other terms are signs of many individuals, such as "human." Whereas Aquinas thought that the common features of humanity shared by Socrates and Plato were real features of the world, Ockham insisted that universal statements are really a summary of the particular judgments we make about individuals. Saying, "All dogs are furry," is a shorthand way of saying, "Lassie the dog is furry, and Spot the dog is furry, and Rover the dog is furry, and so on." There is not some additional reality, in addition to the individual dogs, the form of "Furriness," in which all these dogs participate. Instead, the verbal sign "furry" signifies the mental sign that was formed by numerous experiences with creatures with similar properties. These mental images and the terms attached to them are all we need to explain human thinking. Thus we can do without all the excess baggage of the theory of universals. Hence, there are no universals in things themselves, and neither do any exist in our minds. Instead, there are only mental signs that refer to individuals or groups of individuals and that serve as the tools of thought. We think *about* particulars, but we think *with* mental signs.

In the final analysis, Ockham has reduced the metaphysical problem of universals to simply this question of logic: How can we use general terms and proper names in propositions to refer to individuals? Ockham's nominalism should be distinguished from the extreme nominalism of Roscelin and his school. They recognized only conventional signs in human thought, whereas Ockham recognizes that concepts function as natural signs. Thus, some prefer to call him a "conceptualist" or "terminist."

Since universals do not really exist, God cannot conceive of them either. God can have an idea of what he is going to create, but this is always an idea of a particular individual. If we say God created the human species, God did not have in mind the form of "Humanity." Instead, he had in mind the multitude of distinct individual people, all of whom somewhat resemble each other. That is all there is to the notion of species.

Metaphysics and the Limits of Reason

THE PRIMACY OF THE INDIVIDUAL

The key to Ockham's view of reality is his conviction that the concrete individual is the only true and genuine reality, the only object of scientific study. The world is a world of individuals that have the qualities they have because this is how God chose to create them. If there were eternal essences, these would limit God's power to freely create as he wished. The fact that God created the world gives us no knowledge of what is there or what it is like. Likewise, examining the world does not give us rational knowledge that there is a God. If everything in the world is contingent, then there are no necessary connections that allow us to draw inferences from one thing to the nature or existence of another thing.

CAUSALITY

Ockham's empiricism and his emphasis on the contingency of all features of the world, led him to take a very radical position on the nature of causality. He believed we could know that every event had some cause or other. However, he realized that experience can only give us probability judgments about the relationship between one specific type of cause and a specific effect. Ordinarily, when we say that "X causes Y" we are saying that whenever X occurs it is followed by Y and that some power in X makes it necessary that Y will occur. However, Ockham argues that all that we really experience is a regularity within experience such that when X is present Y is present, and when X is absent Y is absent. We never experience the hypothesized causal power in X nor the alleged necessity of its effect. There may be a causal relation between X and Y as a matter of fact, but it cannot be known with certainty. For example, we observe that when fire is present (X), things become hot (Y). However, apart from experiencing this sequence, the knowledge of fire alone could not tell us its effect. If he had wanted to, God could have arranged it that the presence of fire would be correlated with things becoming cold. Only experience can tell us what to expect from a given cause, and this knowledge is always probable. If there is no logically necessary relationship between X and Y, then God can, on occasion, produce Y without it being preceded by X, as is normally the case. Hence, Ockham's empiricism provides support for his belief in the possibility of miracles. Normally, God maintains the uniformity of nature, and it is the normal, regular sequences that science studies. But if everything is contingent, there is no contradiction in supposing that God could change the normal sequence of events. The contingency of creation casts doubt on our ability to "capture" the structure of reality in our theories—an assumption central to most of the preceding Western philosophical tradition.

THE DECLINE OF METAPHYSICS

The outcome of Ockham's position is that the importance of metaphysics severely diminishes. Logic simply tells us about the relationship between our mental signs and propositions. It cannot give us factual information about the world, because this can only be provided by experience. Ockham's razor dictated that we should not try to explain something *in* the world by speculating about what is *behind* and *beyond* it. He dismissed any explanation in terms of final causes, saying that they are mere metaphors. Applying his standards of evidence, he showed that many of Aristotle's principles in physics and astronomy were not necessary and self-evident and suggested that any given phenomenon could be explained by many different speculative theories. Furthermore, his view of causality had an enormous impact on the rise of modern science. Instead of trying to find the logical relations between things (for there are no logical necessities in the world), the scientist should instead faithfully observe and catalogue only the empirical facts and their regular sequences. This approach had both good and bad consequences for science. It was a helpful corrective to the medieval-Aristotelian tendency to reason about what *must* be the case instead of observing what actually *is* the case. Under the new approach, empirical discoveries were made that would have been overlooked by the older methods. However, cataloguing observations alone would not have given us the powerful laws and theories of modern physics, for (contrary to Ockham) science cannot do without speculation and theorizing. We now know that what we see (the readings of our instruments and medium-sized objects) can be understood only in terms of entities that we cannot observe directly (subatomic particles). Science cannot avoid theorizing about what is behind and beyond the observable facts. Furthermore, in their attempts to mathematically comprehend the world, modern scientists assume (contrary to Ockham) that there are logically necessary relationships in nature.

REJECTION OF NATURAL THEOLOGY

What Ockham has said thus far allows no foothold for natural theology. Since all knowledge of what exists arises from experience (intuitive knowledge), and since we do not have direct experience of God in this life, we cannot prove his existence or attributes. Only faith and revelation can tell us about these matters. Furthermore, his view on causality undermines the Thomistic arguments. If we only know an effect, we can know that it has *a* cause, but apart from past experience of the causes of similar effects, we cannot reason to the nature of an unknown cause. Hence, we cannot reason from our knowledge of the world to the nature of its cause. To make this point, Ockham critically examines the traditional arguments for the existence of God. The only argument he admits might have some value is Aquinas's argument from efficient causality. Although he believes it can be proven that the world requires some conserving cause, he does not think that reason can show that there is only one such cause nor that this cause has the attrib-

utes of the biblical God. Thus, when we rely on natural reason, probability has replaced Aquinas's certainty about metaphysical issues.

Ockham's razor also affected other issues in natural theology besides the existence of God. Whereas philosophers from Plato to Aquinas thought they could prove that humans had a spiritual nature and were immortal, Ockham says we can only know this on the basis of revelation. All we experience are our internal activities and states such as thinking, willing, joy, and sorrow. We have no experience of the spiritual substance that underlies these psychological activities. Thus, we cannot prove that there is a soul, much less that it is immortal.

Moral Philosophy: Radical Voluntarism

With Duns Scotus, Ockham's moral philosophy revolves around the notion of freedom of the will, both human and divine. It is our free will that makes us moral agents. If an action is determined by natural causes, the person is not responsible and can neither be praised nor blamed. Furthermore, it is the will that makes an action morally good or bad. An otherwise good action done from an evil intention is not a morally good act.

Ockham's very strong view of God's omnipotence makes his moral theory extremely radical. If God is all-powerful, then the whole created order is contingent and a product of divine free choice. However, Ockham includes the moral law within the contingent order of the world. Since there is no universal essence of human nature in the divine mind, no unchangeable natural law follows from this essence. Not only could God have created humans any way he chose, but after creating them he could also have created any moral laws for them he chose. Thus, Ockham pushes the tendencies in Scotus's moral philosophy to their furthest extreme. For Ockham, God is not bound by any law or principles. He is free in thought, will, and action, and therefore anything is possible that is not a contradiction. Hence, actions now considered sins, such as murder and adultery, could have been ethically good, and their performance meritorious, if God had willed them so. However, as a matter of contingent fact, such acts are wrong in the current moral order, simply because this is what God has decided. From these examples, there is clearly no way we can reason to the rightness or wrongness of an action by appealing to natural law. We are totally dependent on revelation for ethical conclusions, because this is the only way we can know what God willed.

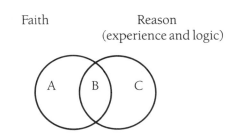

FIGURE 12-1 Thomas Aquinas's model

Summary and Evaluation of Ockham

The ideas Ockham set in motion led to bitter disputes between the realists and nominalists. In 1339 the University of Paris prohibited the use of Ockham's books and in 1340 officially rejected nominalism. More than a century later in 1473, all the teachers in the university were bound by oath to teach realism. However, other universities founded at this time embraced much more freedom of thought and permitted nominalism: Prague in 1348, Vienna in 1365, Heidelberg in 1386, Cologne in 1388.

Ockham's views on the relationship between the various kinds of reality and spheres of knowledge both unraveled the Scholastic synthesis of faith and reason as well as opened the door to the autonomy of science. The difference between Thomas Aquinas and William of Ockham can be illustrated by the circles in Figure 12-1. For Thomas, the spheres of faith and reason were intertwined. The propositions of faith are known through biblical revelation and Church authority. Reason includes all the information that can be gained from our natural cognitive capacities through the combination of experience and logic. Although some truths could only be known on the basis of faith and revelation (A), some of the truths about supernatural things (B) also fall within the domain of philosophy and can be proven by reason. Likewise, truths about the natural world (C) can be arrived at by reasoning about experience.

Whereas Aquinas had announced a marriage between revelation and natural knowledge, Ock-

ham initiated divorce proceedings between them (see Figure 12-2). For Ockham, the truths of theology are completely separate from what we can know through experience or logic. The supernatural and the natural operate in different spheres with different concerns. By means of revelation, faith (A) can give us knowledge about God and spiritual realities. However, it cannot give us knowledge about the world, for given the freedom of God, theology cannot tell us the way that the world is or must be. It is experience (B) that tells us what the created world is like. But from our knowledge of the world, we cannot reason back to God or his attributes because an effect by itself cannot tell us about its cause. Logic (C) is isolated in a sphere by itself and can neither tell us about divine things nor about the world. Logic only tells us about the relationship between propositions. Since reason cannot give us any substantive knowledge about reality (divine or natural), philosophy is almost left without a mission. Ockham's philosophical conclusions attempt to establish the appropriate boundaries between the different spheres of knowledge, but once these are clarified, philosophy can make few (if any) contributions to our knowledge.

In thus drawing the boundaries of knowledge, Ockham's goal was to protect faith from the encroachments of philosophy and science. Faith was in a hermetically sealed sphere unto itself. No argument of the philosophers or new discovery in science could count for or against what the Christian believes. However, in putting theology beyond the reach of reason, Ockham unintentionally freed both philosophy and science to independently pursue their own concerns without the burden of

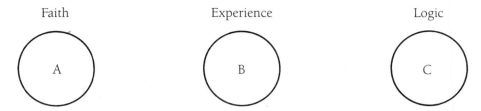

FIGURE 12-2 William of Ockham's model

making their results consistent with theological traditions. Since reason was forbidden to concern itself with matters of faith, it could now concentrate on natural phenomena. In William of Ockham, philosophy was no longer the handmaiden of theology, but took on the new role of being an independent entrepreneur. Although many accused him of being skeptical and of attacking the intellectual foundations of religion, Ockham appeared to have a firm, personal commitment to the Christian faith. However, though his intentions were thoroughly pious, Ockham actually encouraged the secularization of philosophy and science. His emphasis on faith and revelation also influenced the Reformation, as Protestant theologians sought to rediscover the simple doctrines of the Bible, freed from the baggage of theological traditions. One historian says that "for sheer destructive capacity" Ockham was unequaled in this period of time.[7]

CHANGES IN THE METHODS OF SCIENCE

|||

William of Ockham's philosophy set in motion a number of changes in how scientists perceived their task. First, his empiricism emphasized that experience is the key to understanding the world. Second, his methodological "razor" recommended that scientists stick to the facts and do away with all metaphysical speculation. Although this was a helpful corrective to the tendency of medieval scientists to force their observations into the confines of their Aristotelian assumptions, this fear of speculation would eventually need to be moderated to make room for the role of theory in science. Third, Ockham's emphasis on the freedom of God and the contingency of the world actually favored science, even though his position was motivated sheerly by theological concerns. If we can't reason about how the world necessarily *must* be, we can only look and see how God happened to make it.

Ockham's ideas generated a new interest in mathematics, astronomy, and physics by freeing scientists of the burden of making their conclusions consistent with theological and philosophical traditions.

One example must suffice to show how the revolution in science began to take place within the fourteenth century. Medieval scientists had taken for granted (following Aristotle) that the earth was the natural resting place of all terrestrial objects. Thus, they considered it the essence of material bodies to "desire" their natural place. This example shows the tendency of medieval scientists to explain the world in terms of final causes, or the end sought by objects. They knew that bodies accelerate as they fall, but they theorized that as a falling body gets closer to its goal, its natural appetite is increased and it speeds up its journey home. John Buridan (around 1320–1382), a student of Ockham, rejected this answer on an experimental basis. If velocity was merely a function of proximity to earth, then a stone dropped from a tower ought to have the same velocity when it reaches a point 1 foot from the earth as a similar stone at that position that had been dropped from a height of only 4 feet. But obviously, a stone whose starting point was a great height will be moving much faster. A stone dropped from a tower can kill a bystander, but the same stone dropped from a few feet cannot. Accordingly, Buridan developed a new account of the physics of acceleration. Using Ockham's razor, he gave a simpler account of the phenomenon without appealing to final causes or natural ends.

MYSTICISM

Ockham's nominalism and radical empiricism helped support the growing movement of mysticism. If logic cannot tell us about God and we can only know what we directly experience, then instead of trying to *understand* God conceptually, we should strive to *experience* him. Religious mysticism emphasizes that God can only be known through a special kind of religious experience. The typical mystic claims that language and reason are too limited and abstract to adequately comprehend an infinite and transcendent God. Therefore, the mystic seeks to rise above our normal modes of cognition and encounter God in an overwhelming, religious experience. This experience is characterized by an immediate feeling of the absolute oneness of the self with the divine and a sense of peace and bliss. The mystics' claim that they could directly encounter the object of knowledge (God) was the religious version of what Ockham called "intuitive knowledge." Mysticism was a persistent movement throughout most of the medieval period. However, it became much more prevalent toward the end of the thirteenth century. By downplaying the importance of reason and propositional knowledge, it became another force that undermined Scholastic rationalism.

The greatest mystic of this time was Meister Eckhart (1260–1327), a German Dominican. Even though he was very influential, his writings were condemned in 1329, two years after his death. Although he worked from within a Thomistic framework, his metaphysical inquiries were always directed toward the goal of charting the soul's journey toward oneness with the divine. Influenced by the Neoplatonic tradition, Eckhart viewed God as the One, an absolutely transcendent unity.* Since we use definitions and concepts to limit and grasp what we are trying to understand, they are inadequate instruments for apprehending God. God cannot be captured in the snare of reason. The consequences of this conviction may be the reason some labeled Eckhart a heretic. He frequently put forth a thesis and defended it and then turned around and defended its antithesis. Although this gives the impression that he was contradicting himself, he may have been trying to show the impossibility of pouring the divine nature into our limited intellectual categories. To use an analogy, suppose the only color words we had were *red* and *blue*. How would we describe a purple object? We might first say it is red. But this does not quite fit, so then we would describe it as blue. But this is not accurate either. Purple is both red and blue, and it is neither red nor blue. Just as these limited color categories are inadequate to describe the color purple, so Eckhart thought our theological categories were necessarily inadequate to describe God.

When the Church authorities looked at some of Eckhart's bold and exaggerated statements in isolation, they thought he was teaching heresies.

*Notice the similarities of these terms to those of Pseudo-Dionysius and John Scotus Erigena in Chapter 9.

For example, following the Neoplatonists, he says that God is above being or existence, since he is the source of being. Yet in other passages he says God is existence itself. Furthermore, he claims God is not like a craftsman whose product exists outside himself, implying that creation exists as a part of the being of God. When his critics focused narrowly on such passages apart from his other statements, they understandably assumed he was guilty of the heresy of pantheism. However, in other passages he balances out the picture by saying that God and his creation are distinct and that God is above it.

As with any mystic, the goal of Eckhart's theology was not to proliferate ideas about God but to lead the soul to union with God. Below the level of the intellect, in the innermost recesses of the soul, is the human essence, the "spark" that contains the divine image. This is the part of us capable of joining with God in a mystical union.

"God and I, we are one," Eckhart says.[8] Just as fire changes wood into itself, "so are we changed into God."[9] To achieve this unity, we must negate our individuality. We must empty our souls of everything until we know nothing, desire nothing, and have nothing. Just as I cannot give you anything if your hand is closed and grasping something else, so the soul must be open and empty, purged of even the desire for God and eternity, before God can fill it with himself.

Despite his call to rise above the limits of reason, Meister Eckhart always maintained an interest in metaphysical speculation. His followers, however, tended to leave this focus behind and emphasized the more religiously practical and experiential side of his thought. The influence of his religious mysticism has lasted through the centuries. The great Protestant Reformer Martin Luther was so inspired by his writings that he published one of them under the title of *A German Theology*.

THE DECLINE OF MEDIEVAL PHILOSOPHY

We began our discussion of the high Middle Ages in Chapter 10 with a comparison between the soaring structures of the Gothic cathedrals and the intellectual systems of the Scholastics. Once again, the architecture of the times may serve as a metaphor for the developments in philosophy. The Beauvais Cathedral in France was begun in 1247, about the time that Aquinas began his theological studies. With a ceiling that rose to a height of 157 feet, it was to be the ultimate realization of the architects' obsession to thrust their buildings into the skies. However, ten years after Aquinas died (in 1284), the main structural arches of Beauvais collapsed, unable to bear the weight that had been imposed on them. From then on, the grandiose attempts to push church architecture beyond all previous limits were abandoned. Architects became more conservative

and the size of their cathedrals became more modest, as they recognized the limits of our human abilities to penetrate the heavens with our earthbound structures.

Similarly, the influential thinkers in the fourteenth century became convinced of the limits of human reason and their philosophies were correspondingly modest in their aspirations. Nominalism, voluntarism, the separation of faith and reason, Ockham's empiricism, and the rise of mysticism all contributed to the collapse of the "cathedrals of reason" that thinkers such as Aquinas had labored to build. From Ockham's insistence that theology be based on revelation and not on philosophy, it was a short step to reducing revelation to the words of Scripture alone. This was a step taken by John Wyclif and the later Protestant Reformers. In fact, Martin Luther, the great sixteenth-century

Reformer, was deeply influenced by his reading of Ockham. Those who followed after Ockham credited him with replacing the old ways of thinking with the "new way" (via moderna). However, from the enthusiasm of the Ockhamites it would be incorrect to suppose that the achievements of the Scholastics were abandoned on the trash heap of history. An updated Thomism continues on in the twentieth century as a live philosophical movement. Even the philosophers in the seventeenth century, who so desperately wanted to separate themselves from the Middle Ages, still depended on the terminology and conceptions of the age they disdained. For example, Descartes, Spinoza, Leibniz, and Locke were indebted to their medieval predecessors for their arguments for the existence of God as well as their discussions of substance and causality.[10]

For us in the twentieth century, products of five centuries of modern thought, much in medieval thought appears dusty, antiquarian, outmoded, and abstract. Thus, it may be helpful to leave this chapter with some sense of what made the medieval outlook so satisfying for a thousand years. The historian of philosophy W. T. Jones has expressed it nicely:

> Perhaps the principal element of this world view was its sacramental outlook. What made Augustine, Aquinas, and the other medieval thinkers so fundamentally alike was this outlook they shared. What distinguishes the modern mind so sharply from the medieval mind is that modern men have largely lost that outlook and now share the basically secular point of view of the Greeks. To say that medieval men looked on this world as a sacrament means, first, that they conceived this world to be but the visible sign of an invisible reality, a world thoroughly impregnated with the energy, purpose, and love of its Creator, who dwells in it as He dwells in the bread and wine on the altar. Second, it means that medieval men conceived of this world as a sacrifice to be freely and gratefully dedicated to the all-good, all-true Giver. Thus, whereas for us (and for the Greeks) the world by and large means just what it seems to be, for men of the Middle Ages it meant something beyond itself and immeasurably better. Whereas for us

> (and for the Greeks) life on earth is its own end, for medieval men life's true end was beyond this world.
>
> It can hardly be denied that this sacramental point of view was a block to progress—progress in knowledge of how to control the environment and utilize it for this-worldly purposes. To many it seems equally obvious, now that this viewpoint has disappeared, that men have rid themselves of much that was a liability—ignorance, superstition, intolerance. What is not so obvious is that the modern world has also lost something of value. If the sacramental outlook of the Middle Ages manifested itself here and there in what a modern clinician would describe as acute psychopathology, it also manifested itself in serenity and confidence, in a sense of purpose, meaningfulness, and fulfillment—qualities that the modern clinician looks for in vain among his contemporaries.[11]

Questions for Understanding

1. What changes occurred in the period from 1300 to 1500 that either caused or signaled the decline of Scholasticism?

2. List some of the ways in which Duns Scotus's philosophy differed from Aquinas's.

3. What does Ockham mean when he says everything in the world is contingent? What are the implications of this for the project of a metaphysics based on reason?

4. What is "Ockham's razor"?

5. In what ways did Ockham's view undermine Aquinas's natural theology?

6. What are the implications of Okham's voluntarism for ethics? How does it differ from Aquinas's approach?

7. How do Aquinas and Ockham differ on the relationship between faith and reason?

8. How do the outlooks of Aquinas and Meister Eckhart differ?

Questions for Reflection

1. What are some reasons for either accepting or rejecting Ockham's voluntarism?

2. Ockham's philosophy was largely motivated by theological concerns. Nevertheless, briefly

set out some of the reasons his philosophy contributed to the rise of modern science.

3. Reread the quote by W. T. Jones at the end of the chapter. Construct an argument to support the view that the medieval worldview was a more satisfying one than ours. Construct an argument for the opposite conclusion. Which argument do you think is the stronger one?

Notes

1. Quoted in David Knowles, *The Evolution of Medieval Thought* (Baltimore: Helicon Press, 1962), 300.

2. Quoted in Gordon Leff, *Medieval Thought: St. Augustine to Ockham* (Chicago: Quadrangle Books, 1959), 164.

3. Quoted in Leff, 270.

4. Quodlibet 6, Question 6, in *Selections from Medieval Philosophers*, vol. 2, ed. Richard McKeon (New York: Scribner's, 1958), 373.

5. Quoted in E. A. Moody, *The Logic of William of Ockham* (New York: Russell & Russell, 1965), 49.

6. 1 Sent. 3.2, F, quoted in Frederick Copleston, *A History of Philosophy* vol. 3, part 1 (Garden City, NY: Doubleday Image, 1963), 74.

7. Leff, 279.

8. Sermon 6 of the German sermons, trans. Edmund Colledge in *Meister Eckhart: The Essential Sermons, Commentaries, Treatises, and Defense*, ed. Edmund Colledge and Bernard McGinn, *The Classics of Western Spirituality* (New York: Paulist Press, 1981), 188.

9. Ibid., 189.

10. These points are made by Julius R. Weinberg in *A Short History of Medieval Philosophy* (Princeton, NJ: Princeton University Press, 1967), 291.

11. W. T. Jones, *A History of Western Philosophy*, 2d ed., vol. 2, *The Medieval Mind* (New York: Harcourt, Brace & World, 1969), xix.

GLOSSARY

This Glossary contains key philosophical terms set in bold type in all four series volumes. The chapter where the term is first introduced, as well as those where it plays a central role, appear in parentheses. "Introduction chapter" refers to the Introduction of the one-volume work.

Aesthetics (or esthetics)—An area of philosophy that pursues questions concerning art, including the nature and role of art, the standards for evaluating art, and the nature of beauty. (Introduction chapter)

Agnosticism—With respect to a particular issue, the claim that nothing can be known, one way or another, because the evidence is thought to be insufficient to provide us with any knowledge. Hence, the agnostic argues that we must suspend judgment on the issue. Typically, agnosticism refers to the position that the existence of God can neither be affirmed nor denied. (Chap. 21)

Altruism—The claim that people either are or ought to be motivated to serve the interests of others. The opposite of **egoism**. (Chap. 24)

Analytic judgment—A knowledge claim expressed by an **analytic statement**. (Chap. 22)

Analytic philosophy—A twentieth-century movement in philosophy, particularly strong in America and Britain, that approaches philosophical problems primarily through an analysis of language. Also called *linguistic philosophy*. (Chap. 32)

Analytic statement—A statement in which the predicate is contained within the subject (its truth is based on the meaning and relationship of its terms) and its denial results in a logical contradiction, e.g., "All mothers are parents." Contrasted with synthetic statements. (Chaps. 22, 32)

Antinomy—A pair of seemingly reasonable conclusions that flatly contradict each other and hence cannot both be true. Kant used antinomies to argue that reason contradicts itself when it reaches beyond its proper limits in attempting to answer traditional metaphysical questions about the nature of reality. (Chap. 22)

A posteriori—A type of knowledge, statement, or concept whose content and truth are derived from experience. For example, "Water freezes at 32°F" is an *a posteriori* truth. Contrasted with **a priori**. (Chaps. 13, 22)

Appearance—The way in which something presents itself to the senses which is different from how it is in reality. For example, a straight stick in water appears to be bent, even though it really is not. (Chaps. 2, 3, 6, 22, 23)

A priori—A type of knowledge, statement, or concept whose content and truth can be known prior to or independently of experience. For example, some philosophers believe that "two plus two equals four" and "every event has a cause" are *a priori* truths which cannot be proven by experience. Contrasted with **a posteriori**. (Chaps. 13, 22)

Argument—An attempt to establish the truth of a statement (the conclusion) by showing that it follows from, or is supported by, the truth of one or more other statements (the premises). (Introduction chapter, Chap. 5)

Atomism—A metaphysical position originating with the ancient Greeks that claims that reality is made up of numerous, indivisible particles of matter moving in a void. (Chap. 2)

Autonomy—Being one's own authority or rule giver, as opposed to being subject to external authority. In Kant's ethics this is an essential condition for rational morality. (Chap. 22)

Categorical imperative—According to Kant, a command that is binding on all rational persons at all times, which generates universal moral laws. It commands us to always act in such a way that we could rationally wish that everyone followed the principle governing that action. Contrasted with hypothetical imperatives, in which the command applies only under certain conditions. (Chap. 22)

Cogent argument—An **inductive argument** that is (a) inductively strong and (b) has all true premises. (Introduction chapter)

Cognition—Knowledge or the act of knowing.

Cognitive meaning—The informative content of a statement that asserts a claim that may be either true or false. The cognitive meaning of a statement is sometimes contrasted with its emotive meaning, or the emotional attitude it expresses or evokes. (Chap. 32)

Coherence theory of truth—The theory that a true assertion or belief is one that coheres with our entire system of interconnected and mutually supporting beliefs. (Chap. 24)

Compatibilism—The theory that human beings are *both* determined and free as long as their actions proceed from their own, inner choices and are not compelled by an external cause. (Chap. 17)

Conceptualism—The claim that **universals** are mental concepts obtained by abstracting the common qualities appearing in similar particular objects. See **Nominalism** and **Realism**. (Chap. 10)

Consequentialism—See **Teleological ethics**.

Contingent—A contingent event is one that is not logically necessary, for whether it occurs or not is dependent on other events. Similarly, a contingent statement is one whose truth is not logically necessary. It may be denied without asserting a contradiction. (Chaps. 12, 13, 16, 17)

Correspondence theory of truth—The theory that a true assertion or belief is one that corresponds with the fact or state of affairs in reality to which it refers. (Chaps. 27, 33)

Cosmological argument—An argument for the existence of God based on the claim that the universe requires a cause for its existence. (Chap. 11)

Deduction—The form of reasoning we use when we attempt to argue from the truth of one proposition or set of propositions to a conclusion that necessarily follows from those propositions. (Introduction chapter)

Deductively valid—See **Valid**.

Deism—A religious outlook, based on reason, that acknowledges the existence of God and his creation of the world, but denies that God intervenes in the world either in the form of miracles or revelation. Deists argue that the divinely ordered natural laws and reason make both nature and humanity self-sufficient. (Chap. 19)

Deontological ethics—From the Greek word *deon*, meaning "duty" or "obligation." Deontological ethics defines the moral rightness or wrongness of an act in terms of the intrinsic value of the act. According to this theory, our duty to perform an action (or to refrain from doing it) is based on the nature of the act itself and not on its consequences. Kant was a leading proponent of this theory. Contrasted with **teleological ethics**. (Chap. 22)

Determinism—The metaphysical position that claims every event (including human actions) follows necessarily from previous events. (Chaps. 14, 17, 30)

Dialectic—(1) For Socrates, a conversational method for progressing toward the truth, by continually examining proposed answers to a question, repeatedly replacing inadequate answers with more refined and adequate ones. (2) For Plato, it was the philosophical method of rising above particulars and hypotheses to achieve the highest form of knowledge. (3) For Hegel, it is a historical process in which both thought and reality develop as oppositions and tensions are resolved at a higher stage. (4) Marx adopted Hegel's historical dialectic, but changed it into the conflict and development of material forces. (Chaps. 3, 4, 24, 25)

Dogmatism—Asserting a position without providing adequate reasons for its truth.

Dualism—A theory that asserts that there are two irreducible realities, such as mind and body, spirit and matter, or good and evil. (Chaps. 2, 4, 15)

Egoism—(1) Psychological egoism is a descriptive theory that claims people always pursue what they perceive to be their own best interests. (2) Ethical egoism is a prescriptive theory that claims people *ought* to always act according to their own best interests. The opposite of **altruism**. (3) In both of the preceding types of egoism, egoistic **hedonism** identifies pleasure with one's best interests. (Chaps. 6, 14, 27, 28)

Empirical—Related to sense experience.

Empiricism—The theory that knowledge is obtained solely from sense experience. (Chaps. 2, 13, 19, 20, 21, 28, 32)

Epicureanism—A version of **hedonism**, based on the philosophy of Epicurus (341–271 B.C.), which claims that (1) only pleasure is intrinsically good and (2) all pleasures are not to be desired equally, the more prudent and sedate pleasures being the ones that lead to true happiness. (Chap. 6)

Epistemology—An area of philosophy that pursues questions concerning truth and knowledge. (Introduction chapter)

Essence—The defining characteristic of something. That property or set of properties without which it would not be the sort of thing that it is. (Chaps. 5, 11)

Ethical egoism—See **Egoism**.

Ethical hedonism—See **Hedonism**.

Ethics—An area of philosophy that reasons about morality, particularly the meaning and justification of claims concerning right or wrong actions, obligation, moral rules, rights, virtue, the good life, and the possibility of objective morality. (Introduction chapter)

Existentialism—A nineteenth- and twentieth-century philosophy that focuses on the nature and meaning of human existence as understood from the subjective standpoint of the subject. Repudiating the notion of a fixed human nature, existentialists claim that we are continually creating the self. They stress the priority of subjective choosing over objective reasoning, concrete experience over intellectual abstractions, individuality over mass culture, human freedom over determinism, and authentic living over inauthenticity. (Chaps. 23, 26, 27, 29, 33)

Feminism—A movement within philosophy and other disciplines that (1) stresses the role of gender in shaping the patterns of thought, society, and history, (2) focuses on the ways in which women have been assigned roles throughout history that excluded them from the intellectual and political realms, and (3) strives to produce a society that recognizes women and men as both different and equal. (Chap. 34)

Forms—According to Plato, the Forms are the ultimate realities and objects of genuine knowledge. Forms are nonphysical, eternal, known only through reason, and impart intelligibility and reality to things in the physical world that imitate them. For example, Plato believes all circular things (rings, hoops, wreathes) are imperfect representations of the Form of Circularity. (Chap. 4)

Hedonism—The position that claims pleasure is the only thing that has intrinsic value. (1) Psychological hedonism claims that it is a psychological fact that people always strive to pursue pleasure and avoid pain. (2) Ethical hedonism claims that pleasure is what people *ought* to pursue. (Chaps. 2, 6, 14, 28)

Historicism—The theory that everything human is affected by the processes of history, such that any idea can-

not be understood apart from its historical context and is valid only for a particular time, place, and community. (Chaps. 23, 24)

Idea—(1) In general, any object of thought. (2) For Plato, Ideas were another term for the **Forms** (e.g., the Idea of Justice, the Idea of Circularity). (3) For Descartes and Locke an idea was any mental content, which could include sensations (redness, sweetness, heat) or the mind's mental states (doubting, imagining, believing). (4) For Berkeley, ideas and the minds that contained them were the whole of reality. (5) For Hume, an idea was a copy of an original sensation (called an *impression*) that was recalled in memory or the imagination. (Chaps. 4, 15, 19, 20, 22)

Idealism—The theory that reality is ultimately mental or of the nature of a mind. Idealism characterizes the philosophies of Leibniz, Berkeley, and Hegel. Contrasted with **materialism** and contemporary forms of **realism**. (Chaps. 17, 20, 23, 24)

Indeterminism—The theory that some events in the world (particularly human choices) are not the necessary result of previous causes, because these events are either random or the products of free will. (Chap. 30)

Induction—The form of reasoning we use when we argue from what is true of one set of facts to what is probably true of further facts of the same kind. An inductive argument either concludes something about a new case, based on what was true of similar cases, or it arrives at a generalization concerning all cases similar to those that have been observed. (Introduction chapter, Chap. 21)

Inductively strong argument—A successful inductive argument in which the premises, if true, would make the conclusion highly probable. (Introduction chapter)

Innate ideas or knowledge—Mental contents that are inborn or part of the natural content of the human mind and not derived from experience. Their existence is defended by most rationalists and attacked by empiricists. (Chaps. 3, 4, 15, 17, 19)

Intellectualism—The theory that the intellect is prior to or superior to the will. Accordingly, it is claimed that the intellect or reason perceives that certain ends or goals are desirable and then directs the will to achieve them. Theological intellectualism claims that God's intellect first knows that certain actions are either intrinsically good or evil and then he wills that they should be done or avoided. The opposite of **voluntarism**. (Chap. 10)

Intuition—(1) Knowledge that is directly and immediately known by the mind, rather than being the product of reasoning or inference; or (2) the object of such knowledge. According to Kant, humans can have only sensory intuitions. (Chap. 22, 31)

Linguistic philosophy—See **Analytic philosophy**.

Logical atomism—The philosophy of Russell and the early Wittgenstein, which claimed that the structure of language and reality are the same, since language is reducible to elementary units corresponding to the fundamental units that compose the world of facts. (Chap. 32)

Logical positivism—A twentieth-century version of **empiricism** and a version of **analytic philosophy**, which states that (1) logical and mathematical statements are logically necessary statements (**tautologies**) that do not provide information about the world and (2) factual statements are meaningful only if they are capable of being verified in sense experience (**verifiability principle**). (Chap. 32)

Logos—A particularly rich Greek term that has a large number of related meanings: speech, discourse, word, explanation, reason, order. It is the source of many English words such as "logic," "logo," "biology," "psychology." Heraclitus believed that *logos* was the rational principle that permeated all things. The Stoics identified it with God, Providence, Nature, or Fate. Christian writers identified it with God or Christ. (Chaps. 2, 6, 7)

Marxism—The philosophy based on the writings of Karl Marx, which asserts that (1) reality is material, (2) history follows a dialectical pattern controlled by economic forces, (3) each era of history is characterized by conflict between opposing economic classes, (4) history is a **dialectic** in which each economic stage produces its own contradictions, giving way to its successor, and (5) the present stage of capitalism will be overcome by socialism, leading to the final stage of pure communism in which class conflict will be abolished. (Chap. 25)

Materialism—The metaphysical position that claims matter is the only reality. Also called *material monism*. (Chaps. 2, 14, 25)

Material monism—See **Materialism**.

Metaphysical dualism—See **Dualism**.

Metaphysics—An area of philosophy that pursues questions about the nature of reality. (Introduction chapter)

Monism—Any metaphysical position that asserts that there is only one kind of reality. **Materialism** claims that matter is the only reality, while **idealism** claims that it is mental. (Chap. 2)

Monotheism—The belief that there is only one God.

Moral relativism—See **Relativism**.

Naive realism—The belief that the properties we perceive objects to have are the properties that they really do have in the external world. (Chap. 20)

Naturalism—The metaphysical position that claims that physical nature encompasses everything that is real and that all of reality can be completely explained by the natural sciences. (Chap. 33)

Naturalistic fallacy—The fallacy of attempting to derive ethical claims (what we ought to do) from factual claims (what is the case). (Chap. 32)

Natural law—In ethics, the claim that there is an objective moral law, transcending human conventions, which may be discerned by examining human nature. (Chaps. 3, 6, 10, 11)

Natural theology—A discipline within philosophy that attempts to prove conclusions about God based on our natural reason and experience without appealing to revelation. (Chap. 11)

Nihilism—From the Latin word for nothing; the belief that there is no knowledge or truth and, particularly, that nothing has any genuine value, meaning, or purpose. (Chap. 27)

Nominalism—The claim that there are no real, independently existing **universals** and that universal terms refer only to collections of particular things. See **Conceptualism**, **Realism**. (Chaps. 10, 12, 14, 20)

Noumena—Things as they really are in themselves, as opposed to how they appear in experience. Kant claimed that the noumena were unknowable. They are the opposite of **appearances** or **phenomena**. (Chaps. 22, 23)

Occasionalism—The claim that there is no causal relationship between mental events and physical events, but that certain mental events always seem to occur simultaneously with certain physical events only because the occurrence of one is the occasion on which God produces the other. (Chap. 15)

Ockham's razor—The principle that our explanations should always be as simple as possible, avoiding the postulation of unnecessary entities. Named after William of Ockham (c. 1270–1350), whose formulation of this principle was very influential, particularly in scientific methodology. (Chap. 12)

Ontological argument—An argument for the existence of God based on the concept of God's perfection and unsurpassable greatness. The argument was defended by Anselm, Descartes, Spinoza, and Leibniz and attacked by Kant, among others. (Chaps. 10, 15, 16, 22)

Ontology—The study of the generic features of being, as opposed to the study of the particular things that exist. Ontology is concerned with questions such as "What is most fundamentally real?" "What does it mean to exist?" and "What is the structure of reality?" Some writers virtually identify ontology and **metaphysics**, while others view it as a subdivision of metaphysics. Other philosophers, such as Heidegger and Sartre, distinguish their ontology from metaphysics in order to avoid the latter's association with questions about God, substance, and the origin of the universe. (Chap. 33)

Panentheism—The belief that God's being includes that of the world but is not limited to it. (Chap. 31)

Panpsychism—A form of **idealism** that maintains that all of reality consists of multiple centers of experience, such as minds or souls, who have various degrees of awareness. Leibniz called them "monads," and Whitehead referred to them as "actual occasions." (Chaps. 17, 31)

Pantheism—The belief that God and the world are identical. (Chap. 16)

Parallelism—The claim that there is no direct causal relationship between mental and physical events, but that the two series run parallel to each other. Essentially the same as Leibniz's **pre-established harmony** doctrine. (Chap. 15)

Phenomena—Things as they appear within experience, in contrast to how they are in reality. Kant said that this is all that we could know about the world. They are the opposite of **noumena**. (Chaps. 22, 23)

Phenomenalism—The doctrine that all statements about material objects can be completely analyzed into statements about sense data without making reference to any reality external to sensation. This position is the contrary of **representative realism**. (Chap. 20)

Phenomenology—The attempt to describe the structure and contents of consciousness in a way that is free of presuppositions and that does not go beyond what appears to consciousness. Versions were set out by Hegel, Husserl, and Heidegger. (Chaps. 24, 33)

Pluralism—The metaphysical position that claims that there are many kinds of reality. (Chap. 2)

Positivism—The view that all knowledge claims must be limited to observable facts, that only science provides genuine knowledge, and that the role of philosophy is to apply the findings of the sciences to problems of human conduct and social organization. Positivism rejects all metaphysical claims and any inquiry not reducible to scientific method. Advocated by Auguste Comte and John Stuart Mill. The movement was a predecessor of **logical positivism**. (Chap. 28)

Postmodernism—A movement that arose in the late twentieth century, that was influenced by Nietzsche and Heidegger and that embraces **relativism** and **historicism**. Postmodernists seek to unmask what they consider to be the pretensions of reason and the illusions of metaphysics. They repudiate the Enlightenment ideal of seeking for objective, rational truth and they replace the notion of one, true picture of reality with that of multiple, ongoing interpretations. Postmodernism has been particularly influential in literary studies. (Chap. 34)

Pragmatism—A philosophy that stresses the intimate relationship between thought and action. Pragmatists claim, for example, that the meaning of a concept is identical to the practical effects of the object of our conception. Likewise, a true belief is defined as one that will effectively guide action in the long run. (Chap. 30)

Pre-established harmony—The doctrine that events in the world, particularly the activities of the mind and body, do not causally interact, but have been arranged by God from the beginning of time to work in unison like two independent clocks that keep the same time. Leibniz was its most important proponent. (Chap. 17)

Primary qualities—Those qualities of an object that may be represented mathematically such as size, shape, number, quantity, motion, and location. According to Galileo and the early modern philosophers, such as Descartes and Locke, primary qualities represent the world as it really is. Contrasted with **secondary qualities**. (Chaps. 13, 15, 19)

Psychological egoism—See **Egoism**.

Psychological hedonism—See **Hedonism**.

Rationalism—The theory that at least some knowledge is obtained by the mind independently of experience. (Chaps. 2, 4, 13, 15, 16, 17)

Realism—(1) In its contemporary usage, the thesis that reality exists independently of our consciousness of it, in contrast to **idealism**. (2) In ancient and medieval thought: (a) Platonic or extreme realism refers to the claim that **universals** have an objective, independent existence apart from the minds that know them or the individuals that exemplify them; (b) moderate realism claims that universals are abstracted by the mind from objective features of individuals, but that they do not have any reality apart from minds or individuals. (This is sometimes called Aristotelian realism or equated with **conceptualism**.) All medieval versions of realism are in opposition to **nominalism**. (Chap. 10, 32)

Relativism—(1) In epistemology, the claim that there is no absolute knowledge, because different individuals, cultures, or historical periods have different opinions on the truth and all opinions are equally valid. (2) Likewise, in ethics, the claim that there are no objective moral truths, for all moral judgments are said to be relative to the knowing subject and equally correct. (Chaps. 3, 4)

Representative realism—The epistemological claim that the mind is directly acquainted only with its own ideas, but that these ideas are caused by and represent objects external to the mind. (Chap. 19)

Scholasticism—The dominant philosophy of the medieval period in which logic was used to demonstrate the harmony of philosophy and the authoritative writings of the religious tradition. (Chap. 10)

Secondary qualities—According to the early modern philosophers, these are the subjective sensations (colors, tastes, odors, sounds, temperature) produced within us by the **primary qualities** of an object. (Chaps. 13, 15, 19)

Sense data—A term used to refer to the particular, individual impressions received in sensation, such as particular colors, tastes, sounds, odors, and textures. Reference to sense data need not presuppose anything about their cause. (Chap. 32)

Skepticism—The claim that it is impossible to know anything to be absolutely true. (Chaps. 2, 3, 6, 21)

Social contract theory—The theory that the justification of government is based on an explicit or implicit agreement made by individuals among themselves or with a sovereign power (Hobbes, Locke, and Rousseau). (Chaps. 3, 14, 19)

Solipsism—The view that nothing can be known apart from my self and the contents of my conscious experience, usually leading to the conclusion that "only I exist." Finding solipsism to be implausible, philosophers such as Descartes were motivated to find demonstrations of the external world or other minds. (Chaps. 15, 20)

Sophists—A group of educators in fifth-century Athens who taught the skills of rhetoric and argumentation, usually to prepare people for political careers. Most of the Sophists were advocates of **skepticism** and **relativism**. (Chap. 3)

Sound argument—A deductive argument that is (1) **valid** and (2) has all true premises. (Introduction chapter)

Stoicism—The view that we will find happiness only if we resign ourselves to accept whatever may happen in life. Historically, this view was based on the belief that the universe is fulfilling the benevolent purposes of divine providence and that every event is inevitable. (Chap. 6)

Substance—A fundamental and independently existing reality that supports or underlies the various qualities or properties we perceive. Various philosophers who believe in substances disagree over how many kinds there are and what sorts of things qualify as substances. The concept was particularly important in the philosophies of the Pre-Socratics, Aristotle, Descartes, Spinoza, Leibniz, and Locke. (Chaps. 2, 5, 15, 16, 17, 19, 21, 22)

Synthetic judgment—A knowledge claim expressed by a **synthetic statement**. (Chap. 22)

Synthetic statement—A statement in which the predicate adds information to the subject that is not logically contained within it and in which its denial (even if false) does not result in a logical contradiction, e.g., "All mothers are under fifty feet tall" is a synthetic statement. Contrasted with **analytic statements**. (Chap. 22)

Tautology—A statement that is true because of its logical form; e.g., "X is identical to X." (Chap. 32)

Teleological argument—An argument for the existence of God based on the evidence of purpose and design in the world; e.g., Aquinas's fifth argument for God. (Chap. 11)

Teleological ethics—Any ethical theory that defines moral rightness or wrongness in terms of the desirability or undesirability of an action's consequences. Contrasted with **deontological ethics**. (Chaps. 11, 22, 28)

Teleological explanation—An explanation of an event or thing in terms of the end, goal, or purpose it tends to achieve. (Chaps. 4, 13)

Teleology (or teleological)—From the Greek word *telos*, meaning "purpose" or "end." A teleological metaphysics claims that nature exhibits purpose; i.e., events in the world are directed to the fulfillment of some goal. (Chaps. 4, 5, 11)

Theism—The belief that there is one God, who transcends the world.

Things-in-themselves—According to Kant, the contents of reality as they are, independent of the mind's apprehension of them. Identical to the **noumena**. (Chap. 22)

Transcendental—Refers to conditions within the knower which makes knowledge or action possible. Kant's critical philosophy tried to set out the transcendental conditions that enable us to be knowers and agents. (Chap. 22)

Universal—(1) Any general term or concept that refers to a number of particular things that are members of the same group; e.g., "human" is a universal that applies to each member of the human race. Since the time of Plato, there has been a controversy as to whether universals exist in reality, or whether they are mere concepts or words. See **Conceptualism**, **Nominalism**, and **Realism**. (Chap. 4, 10) (2) As an adjective, it designates that which applies to all persons, at all times, in all circumstances, e.g., universal truths, universal moral rules. (Chap. 4, 22)

Utilitarianism—A theory of ethics and a political philosophy built around the claim that a good action is one that creates the greatest amount of good for the greatest number over any other alternative action. (Chap. 28)

Valid argument—A successful deductive argument whose form is such that if the premises are true, the conclusion necessarily must be true. (Introduction chapter)

Verifiability principle—The criterion of meaning developed by the **logical positivists** stating that (1) a factual statement has **cognitive meaning** only if sense experience can provide evidence of its truth and (2) the experiences that would demonstrate its truth are identical to its meaning. (Chap. 32, 34)

Voluntarism—The theory that the will is prior to or superior to the intellect or reason. Accordingly, reason is viewed as merely an instrument for achieving the ends or goals that the will voluntarily chooses. Theological voluntarism claims that God declares an action to be morally good or evil solely on the basis of his free choice, for he is not compelled to do so because of any intrinsic property in the action itself. The opposite of **intellectualism**. (Chap. 10, 12)

I N D E X

INDEX